T0374332

Inspirational Poetry
By Hal E-looya

Volume II

iUniverse, Inc.

New York   Bloomington

Inspirational Poetry By Hal E-looya
Volume II

Copyright © 2010 Hal Gartner

iUniverse books may be ordered through booksellers or by contacting:

iUniverse
1663 Liberty Drive
Bloomington, IN 47403
www.iuniverse.com
1-800-Authors (1-800-288-4677)

ISBN: 978-1-4502-5159-4 (pbk)
ISBN: 978-1-4502-5160-0 (ebk)

Printed in the United States of America

iUniverse rev. date: 8/23/2010

Dedication

This book is dedicated to my two deceased sons:

Neil Thomas Gartner   1957 - 1966

Robert Bruce Gartner 1958 – 1967

And my dear, departed wife:

Martha Bachman Gartner

5/22/1929 – 11/25/2007

GUIDED

In places strange, that are unknown
  Where what you seek, may hide
Get someone who's familiar
  To help you and to guide.

Guidance from our Lord above
  Will sure help you get started
Find out things our great God did
  And why the sea was parted.

So many proverbs and stories told
  With hopes you understand
The mystery of His miracles
  Performed throughout the land.

Advice to live a joyful life
  With encouragement to forgive
You will make ready for His kingdom
  While here on earth you live.

5-16-09

1

THE SAME

Big muscles really count for naught
  Same for the weakling in his nighty
In God's eyes they are all the same
  His love to them, all mighty.

The meek some day will get it all
  Included in His promise
The proof is His and His alone
   Example – doubting Thomas.

Perhaps the phrase called "Haste makes waste"
  Made by those who can not wait
When time is right you are sure to know
  His timing never late.

As hours tick and turn to days
  And days turn into years
Enjoy your time into the years
  With joy, and sometime tears.

5-15-09

FAITH THAT'S STRONG

When you're no longer fast asleep
  You are now controlled by brain
Movements, thoughts and all you do
  A list hard to explain.

Priorities are first in line
  Spur-of-the-moment might take place
Uncertainty is constant
  For all the human race.

You need strong faith in all you do
  To face the great unknown
You'll be prepared for what comes next
  Even when foul winds are a-blow-en.

5-16-09

BABIES

Babies soon will be grown up
  Our children they will be
As adults and on their own
  To make choices when they're free.

Proper training and good advice
  Will help them as adults
What they do and where they go
  With God gets good results.

Not all children know the Lord
  While some don't even care
It's up to us to let them know
  It's up to us to share.

God's word will help them cope with life
  Make all changes that they need
His love and grace will bring much joy
  When planted, is His seed.

5-4-09

HYPOCRISY & CRITICISM

Hypocrisy is everywhere
  And criticism reigns
When demanding what you think is right
  Always disagree or complain.

Self-righteousness is made well known
  Loaded with lots of pride
Seek to get your thoughts revealed
  Want others on your side.

Judging others is the theme
  Comparison, you will make
Don't care what most others think
  If it satisfies your sake.

If God above would act like this
  There would be no grace and love
No arms held wide to welcome you
  To His mansions up above.

4-23-09

MADE PURE

Refined and refined again
  His word will get more pure
Make constant prayer to God above
  When asking for a cure

Only by His grace and love
  He tries to make us better
In time he will reveal what's best
  There will be no "Dear John" letter.

Avoiding sin that temptation brings
  Will cripple Satan's plans
Knowing that our God loves us
  "Our Rock" not shifting sands.

Although we try to be like Christ
  We still sin, then ask for forgiveness
His truth will take our slag away
  Refining is His business.

4-29-09

PARASITE

When you are habitual
  And gouge the food of many
The never-ending gluttony
  And you never spend a penny.

Bugs we know are parasites
  For some people, that title too
Keep on searching for the free-bees
  It might be me or you.

Keep all their money locked up tight
  They never spend a buck
Depending on the other guy
  Like leeches, they will suck.

When at last there is no more
  To feed upon and use
The parasite will fade and die
  Just like a burned out fuse.

4-11-09

SON OF GOD-JESUS

A short time that He lived on Earth
  He had much wisdom of old
Until age of 33
  Many stories that he told.

Lepers He healed
  And made the blind see
Performed many miracles
  That made our doubts flee.

He told of His Father
  In heaven above
All the blessings He gives
  Filled with much grace and love.

On Easter he proved
  That His Father has power
God restored Him to life
  In 3 days, on the hour

So keep this in mind
  And your faith, keep strong
When life here is over
  With Him you'll belong

4-21-09

DISPOSAL

When you hit the low of lows
  Are you ready for disposal
That's the time a loving God
  Offers a proposal.

Listen to the words of Christ
  The message of His Son
Learn to keep faith that's strong
  And remember He's number one.

Keep on adding words of truth
  In time you will have many
Interpret what the Bible says
  The cost not near a penny.

The words were written long ago
  They lasted through the ages
The Bible is the word of God
  Throughout its many pages.

4-9-09

DEDICATION

Dedication and fixation
  Like one go hand in hand
Especially when it comes to God
  As we march in his glorious band

Thankful for his blessings
  His love shines brightly through
When His grace is given
  It makes all things seem new

Time that's spent to honor Him
  Through Jesus Christ His Son
The Holy Spirit is both of them
  We have them all, three in one.

When each day we keep in mind
  How great a God that we know
Remembering his grace and love
  As He puts on his wonderful show.

4-10-09

ILLUSION

Dreamers have illusions
  Of what this world should be
Reality will stop them cold
  Returning from their spree.

Magicians make illusions
  Perform with slight of hand
Tricks of much amazement
  Make magic that is grand.

Quicker is the hand than eye
  Pick live rabbits from a hat
Do risings with no strings attached
  Or fly upon a mat.

Like us, magicians need to pray
  For all things that are rare
Finding that the grace of God
  Will keep them in His care.

4-10-09

MARATHON

We live and run the grace of life
  Seems like a marathon
Petition God in thoughts and prayer
  To make our troubles gone.

Tired, worn and weary
  We must stop along the way
You'll have a great adventure
  In every passing day.

Exercise to keep you fit
  Sure helps to set the pace
Eat good food, get lots of rest
  And finish, not last place.

Asking God to keep you strong
  Included in each prayer
Participate in what seems hard
  The joy is being there.

4-10-09

POLLUTION

Could sin be called pollution
  When your life gets full of it
Overjoyed you have made Satan
  Now that you are in his pit.

There's a need for many changes
  The process may be slow
Pray that god will help you
  To make your troubles go.

When you follow Jesus
  He'll forgive the sins of the past
Washed and cleaned by God's own Son
  A friendship that will last

The Devil is now put in place
  No longer part of you
Pollution is of yesterday
  Enjoyed by many, not a few.

4-8-09

13

OCCASIONAL

Christmas time or Easter
  Or just once in a while
Don't belong to any church
  Cause that's not in their style.

When trouble comes a knocking
  And you're headed for a fall
That is the only time you pray
  And come out of your stall.

If your faith is just luke warm
  The Devil makes his move
Bait that is called temptation
  It's made to fit his groove.

Part time Christians God frowns upon
  His love for them still strong
Fellowship with followers
  Then soon you will belong.

4-10-09

GREED

Hoarding more than you can use
  Enjoyed the sin called greed
Satan sings a happy tune
  When you take more than you need.

Billionaires who own the oil
  Set prices that are high
Some day they will leave their wealth behind
  And be equal in God's sky.

It seems the ones who need it less
  Are those who fill their face
Perhaps a habit formed by greed
  Made them set this pace.

Sharing all your gifts from God
  Should be the golden rule
The Devil likes the greedy ones
  And makes them think it's "Cool."

4-6-09

ON HIGH

Elevation does the trick
  Beats driving in your car
When you're aloft like birds and planes
  Now you can see quite far.

When you're high, all things look small
  Up close they're mighty large
It's good to know that God sees all
  We have the best in charge.

Take my advice get up in height
  And take a look around
Admire God's creations
  His beauty, now you've found.

4-6-09

XENOPHOBIA

Superstitions mixed with fear
  Of all things that we know
Peers that have this problem
  Will make your feelings grow.

Ladders, black cats, shoes on table
  Are many, of a few
Fearful of the great unknown
  Ask "What would Jesus do?"

For reasons that we do not know
  Inside, this fear will lurk
Psychiatrists are baffled
  Why their treatment does not work.

Xenophobia may be last of such
  Of all phobias on the list
Ask in prayer for healing
  In time it will be missed.

12-24-08

17

WISDOM

Understanding situations
That happened in the past
Wisdom how to handle such
 With outcome that should last.

We can't go back and change events
That were no good and bad
If back then we made choices right
Today you would be glad.

Longevity plus experience
Builds wisdom, it will grow
Solving problems others have
Because you have the know.

When you're young you must give thought
What will the outcome be
Seek some help when you decide
 And watch your burdens flee.

12-14-09

INSEPARABLE

Inseparable are blood relations
  Like parents and their kin
Red, black or yellow
  Will have this color skin.

Different races, different colors
  When mixed it's a one of many
Then all white don't have chance
  Few regrets are had, if any.

Our God and Son, inseparable
  We know this for a fact
And upon this earth, father and son
  Find similarity in their act.

All the things that claim this name
  Are bonded close together
That is the way they'll always stay
  Forever and forever.

12-23-08

FEUD

When opposition has no end
  A feud is taking place
Both sides will never listen
  Hold fast to keep the pace.

Their attitude is stubbornness
  They will battle till the end
Society calls them radical
  Their thoughts remain a trend.

Famous names who fit this bill
  The Hatfields and McCoys
Tit for tat, they kill and kill
  And think they're good ol' boys.

Meditation will take place
  Yet they will not concede
Violate the treaty of a peace
  Their action, we do not need.

12-20-08

INTERMISSION

One of two, is half time
  Looked forward to by many
Time to sell refreshments
  You'll spend more than a penny.

Restrooms will be occupied
  This is a fact we know
Intermission gives all comfort
  Now ready for the show.

Half time, players analyze
  And try to fix all wrongs
Hoping that they will score big
  And sing no loser's songs.

12-20-08

CERTIFY

Fraud takes place when checks bounce
  When in doubt they certify
This makes certain funds exist
  For whatever you may buy.

Those who cheat and pass bad checks
  Forget what is called pride
When they are caught they'll pay the price
  And spend time on the inside.

Certified by proof you'll need
  A photo card required
Most businesses will ask for this
  And check for date expired.

When in doubt, must certify
  To make sure you can pay
Credit cards are checked this way
  It takes place every day.

12-20-08

ISOTROPIC

Very few things that share a name
  Can be listed for detections
Isotropic is just one
  The same value in all directions.

Our God is one who does this well
  He's always everywhere
Controls and rules the universe
  With grace and tender care.

Words that are unusual
  Are very seldom used
Now added to vocabulary
  It makes me much amused.

12-24-08

1949 at the Fishing Station where I rented
row boats with my Dog Duke.

INTERNAL MEDICINE

It's on the menu every day
  To keep us well and strong
Lots of pills that don't taste good
  To this group we belong.

They have all different colors
  Some pills in capsule form
Used to keep our crew in shape
  And make us feel like norm.

Dieticians feed us food
  Chock full of vitamins
Tell us that it's good to eat
  Potatoes with their skins.

Some foods people just don't like
  It could be me or you
Disguised, you're sure to get it
  Hid within the stew.

12-19-08

FOILED

Foiled again, we know your tricks
  You fooled us once before
Wearing the armor of our God
  Will keep you from a score.

Your cleverness is put on hold
  Our strength comes from the Bible
Knowing how you play the game
  Will keep us all from libel.

"Tricky Dick," a phrase once used
  For one who would deceive
Made all kinds of promises
  With hopes we would believe.

The truth will keep ole Satan foiled
  Way back in hell he'll burn
Gods message we'll get out to all
  So they're not next in turn.

12-20-08

Heavy

Burdens sometime fill our life
  A heavy load to bear
That is when you need a friend
  To carry loads and share.

It's been told so many times
  We have that friend we need
God sent Jesus Christ to us
  He'll be your friend indeed.

When it's time to pick a friend
  Remember He's the one
Born to carry loads like us
  Because he is GOD'S SON.

Now you know where help is found
  He's ready and He's able
Right away you'll know it's Him
  His love remains HIS LABEL.

12-20-08

Victory

When you want a winner
  And an idol you can follow
Don't depend on peers or friends
  Their choice might just be hollow.

A victory seemed so far away
  The day that Jesus died
That's when our glorious God stepped in
  Wiped tears from those who cried.

It was the way the only way
  To save the world from sin
Restored our Lord brought him to life
  Thus showed us how to win.

Victory we all can have
  Get called home when we die
We're most thankful for his promise
  To live in mansions in the sky.

12-20-08

Ambition

Degrees of satisfaction
  Depends on ones ambition
Smart enough to realize
  Can't happen just by wish-in.

Lazy bones the opposite
  Don't care, just likes to sleep
Watches others run around
  And just prefers to creep.

Ambition is a hyped up thing
  Much effort to succeed
Gets the sheepskin now in hand
  For most jobs he will need.

12-20-08

Harvest Time

We think of food at harvest time
  God thinks of us instead
He knows the Devil inside out
  Satan's lures we often dread.

We're thankful for what's gathered in
  Celebrate and feast at Thanksgiving
All families do this every year
  With those of us still living.

Some places where a storm hit hard
  They gather not too much
Still thankful for little what they have
  Cause God will keep in touch.

12-20-08

Manufactured

Labels tell you where it's made
  What size and how to clean
Found on all the things you buy
  In places where it's seen.

Most times it will say China
  We see this every day
Americans will supervise
  And give out little pay.

Many products that you buy
  Are made in foreign lands
This could be most anything
  Including famous brands.

Unemployment here on the rise
  No unions to defend
In time will get much bigger
  It seems to have no end.

12-22-08

Establishment

Allowing those who disagree
  Is our democratic government
With foes of all society
  They resist and hate establishment.

Skin heads and the K.K.K.
  Are names you recognize
Others that are radical
  Might fool you with disguise.

Some one has to take the lead
  They might be good or bad
Establishment is here to stay
  Some countries wish they had.

Coming to the USA
  Is what most foreigners seek
A mixture from all countries
  Could be the well known Greek.

Those held back want freedom
  Don't care how high the price
Work hard to be American
  And want a life that's nice.

12-20-08

Epidemic

Sin was known throughout the land
  Epidemic like it spread
Nothing stopped this cruel advance
  No fear what some might dread.

The Devil bold and happy
  Lured many to his fold
Those who did not follow him
  Were left out in the cold.

God's truth was used to warm things up
  He put a halt to Satan's fling
Put a stop to all things bad
  And made sinners feel His sting.

Sent His Son to let us know
  That he is still in charge
Through Jesus made His promise known
  His following soon got large.

Protection from catastrophes
  That epidemics cause
Shots that give immunity
  Are given much applause.

12-21-08

Fabulous

Another word describing God
  Can make all followers zealous
When thinking of His blessings
  You can say he's FABULOUS.

Given power to His Son
  Great miracles were performed
Proved He was the Son of God
  At this the Devil scorned.

Along with words of greatness
  Fabulous fits at times
Wonderful amazing awesome
  So many fit that rhymes.

HAL-E-LOO-YA   PRAISE THE LORD

12-21-08

DEPRECIATE

Once was new and now it's used
  Buy a new car and you'll see
Once around the block it's used
  Just watch those dollars flee.

When it's used and had good care
  It still depreciates
Some lucky 2nd hand owner
  Will buy at discount rates.

Everything that one might own
  Is subject to this fate
Value drops, it will in time
  You'll see, if you just wait.

Built in obsolescence
  Will make it soon "NO GOOD"
Costly to replace it
  This cycle understood.

12-17-08

TRANQUIL

Alone in prayer you'll hear His voice
   Could be most anywhere
Those who love the great outdoors
   Know what He has to share.

Tranquility, with God, alone
   The time with Him is well spent
Then you'll feel His love and grace
   Know what His message meant.

One on one is tranquil time
   Will make you feel His love
Jesus tells us of great things
   That his Father has above.

12-17-08

DESOLATE

Sins piled up, like debts man owed
  The outlook did seem sad
Desolate, tired and weary
  His happenings were all bad.

This situation was wide spread
  God saw the need for change
Sent His Son to make things right
  To free and rearrange.

Desolate souls need Jesus
  To lift them from despair
Teach them of God's love and grace
  And tell them of His care.

Jesus gave his life in sacrifice
  To prove what God can do
Paid our debts, with the blood He shed
  Soon followers grew and grew.

12-12-08

COLOSSAL

When you think of something big
   Comparison comes to mind
The universe will come to life
   Since God made all you'll find.

Colossal, huge, giant
   Humongous says it's large
Description of this monstrous thing
   Once kept in your garage.

The news will say colossal
   This makes you pay attention
When there is much damage
   Others terms, they're sure to mention.

When colossal is your attitude
   You never will think small
Remembering what did take place
   And how much you can recall.

12-19-08

MONOTONOUS

Having all the things you need
  And God does not get credit
This could be a foolish move
  In time, he's sure to edit.

Solomon had everything
  Women, wine and money
Had all things that one could have
  His life, then sweet like honey.

Monotony then soon set in
  What he had seemed naught
Let others know just how he felt
  His message was well taught.

Temptation filled with glitter
  Is the life of movie stars
Change their mate quite often
  They do the same with cars.

Monotony will be on hold
  Some goals we may achieve
Our happiness is grace and love
  Cause His will is to believe.

12-12-08

MICROSCOPIC

Compared to our surroundings
  We may seem microscopic
Magnified by intelligence
  Describes us in this topic.

"East is East and West is West"
  When distant, things look small
We're specks that move and have control
  On this celestial ball.

Germs are microscopic
  Enlarged when magnified
Through small, they will become immune
  To medication when applied.

We call them microscopic
  Cause the naked eye can't see
Praise the Lord, they're out of sight
  No need for us to flee.

12-12-08

RADICAL

At times man seems to be more radical
  Once good is now deemed bad
Daily changes how he thinks
  Could make him sad or glad.

From one extreme or maybe two
  His restless mind keeps going
Experiments on everything
  To keep us all in knowing.

Good treatments now for illnesses we have
  'Til now, did not exist
Could enhance your breathing
  With a special kind of mist.

Behavior of the radical man
  In time he'll find a cure.
Technology that's installed by God
  Will help to make us pure.

12-12-08

KING JAMES

Translation of the Bible
  By King James the 1st of England
Still remains the standard
  Throughout England and our land.

Greeks and Jews had all the facts
  With these and thous back then
Printed words to read more clearly
  Much better than a pen.

Presentation is the key
  The facts will still remain
Maps and guides with study plans
  Are used world wide to train.

12-12-08

PREVAIL

What we do and how we think
  Succeed and sometimes fail
Needing more than what we have
  With God we will prevail.

Technology has limits
  Still man has his quest
A thirst that must be satisfied
  Before he'll stop to rest.

Forging on with constant prayer
  A dream that must be filled
Flirting with the great unknown
  Could get a person killed.

Confident that God will help
  He'll give it one more try
Persistent, HE WILL NEVER QUIT
  Most people just say WHY?

12 -11-08

METICULOUS

Everything must be in place
  All clutter since removed
Possessions now are neat and clean
  All slippery things are grooved.

Getting dressed with clothes that match
  Precise in your selection
Things that need your loving care
  Are given much affection.

Hired help will mess things up
  This happens with good intention
When they leave I'll rearrange
  No comments will I mention.

Habits formed so long ago
  Meticulous got its start
Finding best, where it looks neat
  Accomplished if you're smart.

12-11-08

JEALOUS

Wanting what some others have
  Your attitude is zealous
Affection that you'd like to have
  Could mean that you are jealous.

Depending on ones self control
  The boiling point is near
Emotions play a great big part
  Enough to shed a tear.

If when you stop to realize
  How God made none the same
Jealousy will take a hike
  And put out that old flame.

12-18-06

MODIFY

Make a change, just add or take
  To find out what you desire
Rearrange 'til satisfied
  What's left, goes in the fire.

Leave well enough alone, I say
  When working good is reached
It can't get no better
  Don't modify, I preached.

Not all things need fixing
  Since most will work just fine
Tinker and you'll break it
  I'll warn you, one last time.

12-19-08

GULLIBLE

Those who fool the innocent
  And cause them lots of trouble
Hide the truth in tiny print
  Because they think we're gullible.

Lessons learned about these scams
  Could cost to some degree
All false adds they advertise
  Are aimed at you and me.

Fool me once, I hope not twice
  You caught me unaware
CAUTION, when it sounds too good
  This info I will share.

Convincing statements make you think
  The offer is legit
Show you how to save a buck
  To develop a buying fit.

12-18-08

OUTLOOK

When all things are analyzed
  At times the outlook is grim
That's the time to pray to God
  Since all blessings come from Him.

Foolish fun don't last that long
  If Satan has his way
Pick your home and realize
  In heaven or hell you'll stay.

When confused or have your doubts
  You need God's reinforcement
Words of wisdom and advice
  Are found in both the New and Old Testament.

  Once dim, your outlook now is bright
    Now feelings sure and bold
  How you had this turn about
    All others should be told.

12-18-08

WATCHFUL

Taking care of things held dear
  Is filled with TLC
Watched eyes that fill the needs
  Much help to them will be.

Possessions will last longer
  When proper care is done
Energy that is spent this way
  Should be a lot of fun.

The owner is responsible
  Most watchful they must be
Time well spent is time worth the cost
  It could be a pet or tree.

12-11-08

1963 Honda Dream motorcycle,
the year I quit smoking.

HERBICIDE

The Bible is a herbicide
  To kill the weeds in life
Cutting into the mindful soul
  With words sharp as a knife.

Wisdom, lessons, good advice
  It covers everything
The outcome of man's sinful ways
  In offerings, what to bring.

Stories told, are gospel truth
  Who lived on earth at the time
Stones were used in punishment
  Disobeyers were changed to brine.

Read it once or maybe more
It has the Godly trend
The words will have more meaning
As we try to comprehend.

12-12-08

COMPULSION

Feeding on compulsion
  The Devil makes his bid
Remembering "PANDORA'S BOX"
  Trouble lurks behind the lid.

"Curiosity killed the cat"
  You heard that said before
Venture in more sinful acts
  You'll make the Devil score.

Urged by your compulsion
  All else is put aside
Fallen from you know what's right
  You'll lose what you called pride.

Getting back to facts you know
  The truth, the light, the way
With these in mind, compulsion fades
  And you'll have a brighter day.

12-11-08

INTERCEDE

Minding not your business own
  You butt in with a plead
Hoping to make a settlement
  Is why you intercede.

Opposing views will always be
  The best way, split in two
Decisions need a compromise
  To help more than a few.

Intercession will take place
  To settle a dispute
When the bottom line is formed
  The outcome soon will root.

12-11-08

INFERIOR

Those who classify themselves
  Much lower than the rest
This complex is inferior
  God rates you with the best.

Comparing self to those with talent
  Could make you feel this way
You alone have hidden charms
  To make all others sway.

Looks sometimes can cause this plight
  Remember, "beauty is just skin deep"
Be reassured personality reigns
  And get a good night's sleep.

12-11-08

INCOMMUNICADO

Vocal understanding
  Is still when you can't hear
Although the volume is quite loud
  The message is not clear.

Incommunicado
  Of most the spoken word
Conversations don't make since
  Mixed up, that you once you heard.

Hearing aids can amplify
  Which does not mean its clear
When the loss is very great
  Some words you'll never hear.

Seeing words that match the tone
  Seem to be a help
Feedback caused by who knows what
  With whistles, or a yelp.

Those who know the problem
  Will speak loud and slow
Hoping you will understand
  What they want you to know.

12-7-08

INSTITUTIONS

Treat the sick in hospitals, incarcerate in prison
  A special place for the deranged
A secure place to house them
  Their life perhaps has changed.

Some institutions paid by taxes
  While others have a fee
Treatments for their problems
  Perhaps one day will flee.

Society established these
  To keep us well and free
Functional in rising cost
  We will have to wait and see.

12-11-08

DISCOURAGED

Despondent, depressed and discouraged
  This calls for needed prayer
Give God your utmost troubles
  He's there with grace and care.

In time he will make all things right
  According to His will
Upset emotions He will calm
  And at His grace, you'll thrill.

Human beings feel this way
  Because of what takes place
God knows how to handle this
  And put a smile upon your face.

12-11-08

S.O.S

International call for help
  "Save our Souls" is used
Those close by will heed the call
  It's never been abused.

Danger and life threatening
  SOS is used at sea
Know that, if help soon doesn't come
  The end of life could be.

Dots and dashes of Morse code
  Or radios make this call
Location must be added
  When sinking in a squall.

Rescued souls have God to thank
  Your life it did not end
By his grace, you'll sail once more
  Your understanding friend.

12-7-08

AVERAGE

Primitive man, most hostile then
  Was known to be a savage
In time domestication took place
  And now he's known as average.

Classified as a middle man
  He's not too bad or good
Average you could call him
  This title understood.

Don't know how you will fit in
  Your standard must be rated
Can not use what we once could use
  That system is out dated.

Some are rich , some are poor
  With average in between
Uncle Sam says how much tax
  He'll make your savings scream.

12-7-08

GUESTS

Friends who join in meals we share
  Are picked from all the rest
Invited to do what we do
  While here, they are our guest.

Friends need friends to make this so
  Most times its give, not take
This could be some long lost pal
  It's done for goodness sake.

Shepherds came when Christ was born
  They knew that He was blessed
Mary and Joseph did not mind
  These uninvited guests.

Depending who is host
  The guest is you or me
What future holds tomorrow
  The meal then could be free.

12-7-08

SAFETY

All the errors and mistakes
  Now are safety rules
Things that really happened
  Acts done by thoughtless fools.

Knowing that one could get hurt
  Safety takes first place
ATV instruction books
  Is stressed on, not to race.

Hours of work are lost each year
  A drain on compensation
Suffering from these accidents
  Include those of relation.

Keep in mind WHAT NOT TO DO
  Much joy can still be yours
Violate, do foolish things
  Safety rules don't have any flaws.

12-4-08

PRESIDENT

Elected by his peers to serve
  He rules at each event
This will hold for 4 long years
  This is your PRESIDENT.

Improvement on so many things
  He'll try to make us better
Promises that must be filled
  We hope it is to the letter.

Diplomats from around the world
  Reply on what he thinks
Busy is his schedule
  No time for 40 winks.

Congress and the Senate
  Will vote on what takes place
On all the whys and wherefors
  Of our troubled human race.

Criticism there will be
  Opinions make this so
When at war, that he declares
  In the Service we will go.

12-5-08

UNSEEN

Those who work real hard at times
  To keep things nice and clean
These busy bees who do the job
  Most likely are unseen.

Hopefully, they will get paid
  For what they do, well done
Jesus did so many good things
  Now unseen is God's son.

"Seeing is believing"
  No need when you have God
He's there when you're in trouble
  He is your lighting rod.

Miracles, not magic
  Performed by the power of prayer
Love and grace, is what He gives
  His subjects get His share.

12-1-08

PEOPLE WHO CARE

People see I am disabled
  Open doors, even when I am able
Such kindness I don't expect
  Their aid somehow I could detect.

Generosity still is here
  Much consideration is shared
This makes me feel good
  To have people who really cared.

It is good to know
  That God's creatures do this
Now Satan will surely frown
  Another soul he's sure to miss.

Every good turn, I appreciate
  It comes from God's own will
Later in life, this could be you
  To enjoy what I now thrill.

12-3-08

EASY

Declared, to not be difficult
  Easy is your quest
Simplified for everyone
  You're sure to pass the test.

Diagrams that come with toys
  Are easy to assemble
Sometimes how to make it work
  Confusion makes you tremble.

"EASY DOES IT" good advice
  From those who wish you well
Some directions that don't make sense
  Could be written down in hell.

When you buy a toy that is boxed
  Please read what's on the label
Pay someone who knows just how
  It's worth it, if he's able.

12-4-08

ROUTINE

Eat all meals at given times
  Get sleep when time is right
Action, the same in most things done
  With time to rest at night.

Now and then you need a break
  To differ from routine
Time is spent on each event
  You'll have things nice and clean.

Good habits are formed by this
  Preventing, hit and miss
Overdone, could be a bore
  Take breaks and don't insist.

Now and then forget this role
  Go fly the coop, your goal
Routine has its time and place
  TOO MUCH you'll pay the toll.

12-4-08

POSITIVE

Make no changes
  Take or give
Means just one thing
  You're positive.

All the facts can claim this name
  It answers all the whys
Deviations don't exist
  When viewed with one's own eyes.

Miracles by JESUS CHRIST
  Made positive in life
Those he healed are living proof
  Now banished is their strife.

Word for word made positive
  Inspired by God was written
His Bible pulls no punches
  Advice to those once smitten

12-4-08

VACANCY

Signs out front of all motels
  Says "NO" when they are filled
All of them want cash up front
  For this you're never billed.

Depending on the time of year
  Or what is taking place
Reservations guarantee your spot
  Making sure you'll have that space.

Heaven don't have any signs
  By grace, it's YES or NO
Hopefully it will be yes
  When it is time to go.

Vacancy is up to you
  You must believe and follow
Trust in Christ, is all it takes
  His promises are not hollow.

12-4-08

CONFLICT

Conflict has reigned upon this earth
  Many places, much unrest
Yet we have a God in charge
  That keeps his followers blessed.

Cain and Abel disagreed
  It only takes just two
Wars continue everywhere
  Involves more than a few.

Rebel to those who have control
  Who gathered wealth and power
Equal rights for those put down
  A new rule, soon to flower.

A never ending stream of wars
  No telling where they'll be
Big countries try to mediate
  We'll just sit tight and see.

12-3-08

BEAUTY

Beauty they say, is just skin deep
  Personalities share that name
People, just like snow flakes
  None are quite the same.

Grouchy, selfish, self-proclaimed
  They play with Devil toys
Concerned only for their needs
  Their attitude annoys.

Crippled, homely or defiled
  Our God still loves them all
Only by his grace I go
  Are words you may recall.

One day maybe these poor souls
  Will come to know God's love
And share his Son's great sacrifice
  And live with Him above

12-3-08

SHOPPING

When you shop, you hope to find
  The perfect thing in mind
Sometimes not affordable
  Have to take another kind.

Prices seem outrageous
  On some things that you buy
Quality will charge you more
  On that you can rely.

Bargain stores keep prices down
  Rates formed by competition
Scouts go out and check on this
  It seems to be tradition.

Many hours are spent by those
  Who want to save a buck
Sometimes they will make a find
  And sometimes, out of luck.

12-3-08

DECORATIONS

Decorations make things bright
  Each different, for each season
Stars and angels top the trees
  To celebrate Christ, the reason.

Halloween, you will see pumpkins
  Big feast, Thanksgiving day
Christmas brings us Santa Claus
  Many presents on his sleigh.

Stars and stripes with fireworks
  To celebrate the 4th
After Santa's busy night
  He goes back home, up north.

Decorations put you in the mood
  For each seasonal event
These times are made more meaningful
  The time and effort is well spent.

12-3-08

Mother, sister Louise and I in Rockaway, Arverne, Long Island, NY 1930. I'm in the sailor suit, age 5. Taken at the back of the first place we lived that was in a row of 8 bungalows.

IDEAL

You have ideal conditions
  Know God is on your side
Joy reflects in your attitude
  Now you have a place to hide.

Troubles will not seem so bad
  Knowing of His grace
You will be a winner
  When you finish every race.

Anticipation makes you feel young
  Even when you're getting old
Waiting for that final day
  When His heaven will unfold.

So when the situation
  Don't seem to be ideal
Remember what He promised
  In His heaven, all will heal.

12-3-08

TALENT

Talent is God given
  Perhaps you are endowed
Some excel in what they do
  And stand out from the crowd.

Good at sports, or maybe crafts
  Learned to play an instrument
Since good, at your occupation
  It does more than pay your rent.

With field that is wide open
  Variety, yours to pick
If magic is your talent
  You amaze in every trick.

Olympics bring on talent
  They come from round world
Top talent win gold medals
  Country flags are then unfurled.

12-3-08

NEWS

Unrelated happenings
  Will make most of us confused
Unless it's featured on T.V.
  With all updated news.

Happenings around the world
  Of who did what and why
Sad stories, full of grief and woe
  Make tears flow, when you cry.

Most big news, are things gone wrong
  To this, most pay attention
Good things, don't make a great headlines
  They hardly get a mention.

Those in charge, tell what you see
  They pick from what seems best
If you want the total news
  Some stations have the rest.

12-3-08

BLESSINGS

Blessings come in many forms
  Perhaps not what expected
His final choice is what takes place
  He needs not to correct it.

Most the time, we don't know why
  What seems unfair decisions
When a family is wiped out
  The cause, head on collisions.

Young or old, you have no choice
  Of when He calls you home
Enjoy his blessings until then
  No matter where you roam.

12-3-08

MERRY CHRISTMAS

I'm Elmer the elf
  I make lots of toys
And fill up the shelf
  For the good little boys.

Ma Santa Claus
  Will take care of the girls
She has many presents
  As a list she unfurls.

Santa's red underwear
  Is now nice and clean
Mrs. Claus took it from
  The washing machine.

His red suit is off
  To the tailor it went
He'll wear it next year
  If others don't rent.

He says HO! HO! HO!
  To his reindeer, he talks
When they won't pull his sleigh
  Then surely, he walks.....

He'll come down the chimney
  And fill up your socks
And if you're not good

You might get just rocks.

It's back home to rest
  After one busy night
He'll shout MERRY CHRISTMAS
  And wish all A GOOD NIGHT.

12-3-08

RESPONSIBLE

Responsible are the ones
  Who have things in control
For now they have the power
  Protection is their role.

Just how long they hold this claim
  Depends on what they do
In their care for anything
  It could be me or you.

Transportation to and from
  It helps to fill our needs
Safety comes up number one
  When you perform these deeds.

12-1-08

DETAILS

All the whys and where's
  A story short or long
Suspense until the climax
  A sad or happy song.

Details given step by step
  To some might be a bore
Then again most others
  Look for more and more.

Some might go into details
  To keep your interest high
Books that feature mystery
  Because of this you buy.

Motor mouth, give all details
  They don't know when to quit
If they keep on talking
  It could cause a detail fit.

12-1-08

LOST

Wandered in the woods too far
  Surroundings look so strange
Looks as if I might be lost
  My bearings must arrange.

Darkness is no time to act
  Must settle in till dawn
Warmth and shelter out of pine
  Don't want to be forlorn.

Boy Scout training helps a lot
  Must use what one can see
A makeshift shelter out of pine
  The bedding from a tree.

Build a fire, and eat what's left
  Tomorrow you'll think clear
Compass and map will get you out
  Not thinking got you here.

11-30-08

FOREVER

Forever is a long time
  On earth it has no end
Love is the one thing you can do
  Such feelings need no mend.

Heaven is not like here on earth
  I'm sure there are no clocks
Joy they say, is being there
  Safe, high upon his rocks.

Salvation got you here at last
  You come here by God's grace
United with the ones you love
  His kingdom now your place.

Years may seem like moments
  Ten thousand, maybe more
Forever and forever
  Is what you have in store.

11-12-08

EXPLORE

Toddlers like to look around
  They'll open every door
Inquisitive to know all things
  Their quest is to explore

Imagination lights their fire
  Not knowing what they'll find
Adventure, danger, who knows what??
  Could be most any kind

Out in space, or ocean deep
  Which one will he chose??
Keep on trying, one more time
  His quest is win or lose

11-12-08

HEAVEN

The sun is always shining
  There is no need for sleep
Enjoy the freedom of no pain
  On earth you had to creep.

That's what He says is heaven
  Our God and Son proclaim
Forever with your loved ones
  That's where you will remain.

Sorting out who He takes home
  By grace we're on that list
Left behind, are many souls
  Some how His words they missed.

When you leave this world behind
  What memories will you leave
Did you try to be a friend
  And try not to deceive?

Welcome friend, a job well done
  Is what you'd like to hear
Enjoyment now forever
  Your life now full of cheer.

11-15-08

CULT

Those who should know better
  Speculate, to find a God
Often join an offbeat group
  That is their lighting rod.

This clan has education
  Don't believe, we know what's true
Rely on someone who justifies
  And tries to make things new.

They follow another human
  Who might have good intentions
This person takes the written word
  And puts it in dimensions.

The Bible makes it simple
  Rely on Jesus Christ
He is the way to heaven
  Why wonder, and think twice??

11-15-08

TEMPTATION

Jesus is our rudder
  To keep us going straight
At times we seem to get off course
  He's there, and never late.

The fast pace world we live in
  Is loaded with temptation
The Devil looks for openings
  Even when we are on vacation.

So keep your Bible close at hand
  And on his path, you'll stay
When pointed in the right direction
  You'll keep temptation far away.

11-15-08

STILL LOVED

The world declares us rubbish
  If we're down and deep in sin
These poor lost souls, our God still loves
  Perhaps their faith will win.

A second chance, His third and fourth
  In time they may respond
Patient is our Holy God
  He waves no magic wand.

This useless group seems fruitless
  Until just one will see the light
Soon to know God loves them
  The winner of each fight.

Someday you will tell others
  How we rose from sin
Perhaps you'll find a hopeless one
  And show them how to win.

11-15-08

911

To make a devastating blow
  It must be by surprise
That is the way it happened
  Right before your eyes.

The enemy took advantage
  Of our unsuspecting plight
Volunteers who lose their life
  Are heroes, in their sight.

Plans to destroy historic places
  4 were on that list
Thanks to those on Flight 93
  Washington was missed.

Hate – the motive, of what took place
  Made plans for this event
Found all ways to get control
  Much time and effort spent.

Took lessons, how to fly our planes
  The weapons of their needs
Helped to build their confidence
  To perform their evil deeds.

Arrangements made that followed
  The blow of 911
Void the threat of enemies
  Moved up to number one.

9-11-08

HALLOWEEN

Funny faces, all dressed up
  With hopes to fool the best
"Trick or Treat," is what they say
  And hope you don't protest.

Kids from 2 to 90 enjoy this holiday
  Costumes worn by young and old
Make Halloween much fun
  With many spooky stories told.

Over flowing shopping bags
  Full of trick and treat
Candy that will last awhile
  If you limit what you eat.

10-31-08

ALONE

When there's no one else around
  To hear me when I groan
The fact of no other human there
  You might say that I'm alone.

Thoughts of what the future is
  Most times, in position prone
The spirit of the Holy Lord
  Is with me, from His throne.

Quiet time with our great God
  Assurance from His word
Ears that hear, when eyes are closed
  Give strength when they are heard.

Be still and listen for His voice
  Direction, plain and clear
When His voice is silent
  Keep his Bible, close and near.

11-16-08

RELIGION

Religion is a subject
  Most people will not debate
Approached in ways of reasoning
  All claim our God is great.

Why a touchy subject??
  The best, is none like mine
All denominations you can name
  Make same, the bottom line.

Catholic, Jew or Baptist
  Believe in just one God
When it comes to Heaven
  Say theirs will get the nod.

Maybe Yes— maybe No????
  In time, I 'm sure you'll know
Until then, some may change their mind
  It's up or down below.

11-15-08

OUR FIRST 100 YEARS

Today's the day we celebrate
  A time for joy and cheers
The Baptist church in Fassett
  Our first one hundred years.

It took a few who loved the Lord
  With Bibles in their hand
A building formed, with steeple grew
  Now sits on hallowed land.

Each pastor through the years gone by
  Have helped to set the pace
Up to now, the present time
  We're thankful for His grace.

His timing surely is the key
  We know that all too well
When time was right he showed his might
  Enter pastor Don Rockwell.

We pray the future of the church
  Ask God's blessings to unfold
He keeps our spirit sound with faith
  Each day that we grow old.

We thank you God for your dear Son
  To you give all glory
Without our Christ, without our God

There would never be this story.

HAPPY BIRTHDAY FASSETT

ROVING EYES

When you reach the golden years
  Live on with hope and trust
Remembering those youthful days
  Do eyes still rove with lust??

Most attitudes are put on hold
  Aside from days gone by
Once more aroused by what you see
  Your thoughts take off, and fly.

This could be declared a sin
  Depending how you dwell
Encouragement from Satan
  Is a ticket to his hell.

10-23-08

ADVENTURE

Much unrest in a dormant stage
  Need a change to feel alive
What will the next adventure be?
  Take all risks and still survive.

It must be new and different
  Restricted to your age
Sky diving with the younger set
  Might seem to fill your rage.

Something that you've never done
  In youth it passed you by
Longing for the thrill you seek
  With thoughts, you still might try.

10-30-08

IMPERVIOUS

Some people are impervious
  To all things that surround
Take advantage of the humble folks
  Make safe while others drown.

Choices made, our God allows
  In time He'll ask you why
Forgiveness is you sentence
  If left out, now you will cry.

Jesus is God's example
  Concerned with love and grace
Sent to earth, to spread the truth
  To all the human race.

Finding those who act like this
  Will put you to the test
Spread the word that gave you joy
  Your effort will be blessed.

10-22-08

AN EXAMPLE

Over doing what is good
  Might lead to some resent
A time and place for everything
  Make efforts called well spent.

"Variety is the spice of life"
  While keeping God in mind
Take interest in what others do
  Perhaps you'll make a find.

Avoid a domineering role
  Let others have their say
Leaders soon will lose respect
  When it's nothing but MY WAY.

  Understanding how you give or take
    Will shine as an example
  Consider what is yours to share
    Take time to find what's ample.

11-2-08

GOLDEN YEARS 2008

We're here from Residential Care
  In a town called Licking
Gone are the days of our youthful ways
  When we did all high kicking.

Still young enough to stir the crowd
  In what we used to do
Acrobatics put aside
  We hope to still please you.

Aches and pains can't slow us down
  We've taken Tylenol
We'll practice for this great event
  Which takes place every fall.

10-21-08

DISCABOBELED

Discabobeled all mixed up
  Some times that's how we feel
Can not focus or concentrate
  On what is fake, or real.

"Haste makes waste," take time to think
  'Til you return to senses
Orchestrate priorities
  Soon rightful ways commence.

Burning candles at both ends
  Could cause this situation
Time out, regroup, get organized
  No need for more detention.

10-21-08

My years as a police officer for the The Port of NY and NJ Authority where I served from 1952 – 1973.

SPECTACULAR

Spectacular, the miracle
  Christ was made alive again
No more pain or agony
  When crucified back then.

Proof for all the doubters
  That God could make this be
He visited all his followers
  Showed scars that all could see.

Now He reigns in Heaven
  Close by his Father's side
There to greet those from the earth
  To all who did abide.

10-19-08

PERSPIRATION

Not like dogs, their tongue hangs out
  To cool off we perspire
Sweaty brows when heated up
  Drenched clothes put out the fire.

When it's hot in summer time
  Much perspiration flows
This takes place in winter
  From exertion when it snows.

Lots of salt and smell can accumulate
  A wash down you will need
Once again acceptable
  When you sit and feed.

10-21-08

ORIGINATOR

Who made it known or invented it
  Is deemed originator
A patent holds for 17 years
  To prevent a duplicator.

Profit known as royalties
  Depends on how it's used
Improvements are most welcome
  And never are refused.

Copyrights are much the same
  The author now protected
Music books and written things
  Made safe, so not detected.

The original originator
  His only Son He sent
To take away much sin we had
  And straighten rules we bent.

10-05-08

TRUE STORIES

Mathew, Mark, Luke, and John
  They tell us truths in story
How Jesus lived upon this earth
  And how He reigns in glory.

Recorded birth at Christmas time
  And why He came to earth
They describes his crucifixion
  And what He did from birth.

Each relate the well known facts
  With the same each bottom line
Why God sent his Son to us
  And why He is divine.

Gospel truths for all to read
  The Bible tells it well
Followers believe what's true
  And pray with him they'll dwell.

10-16-08

ENTERTAINMENT

Relief from work and all life's stress
  Should be a time well spent
A break from what is called routine
  Like living in a tent.

Entertainment comes in many forms
  Watch sports or see a show
Any thing that frees your mind
  Vice-versa highs and lows.

Story books and magazines
  Reveal the authors zeal
Performers have abilities
  Their acting seems like real.

Entertainment is a field that's large
  It includes so many things
All events are held in place
  Until the fat lady sings.

10-19-08

ESTABLISHMENT

The world is God's establishment
  Recorded in the Bible
Theories how it all began
  Will lead to what is libel.

Evolution tells the tale
  That we evolved from apes
Adam and Eve are put aside
  Like wine that's made from grapes.

God made many creatures
  Formed man just like Himself
Made all things that live and breathe
  Imagination bred the elf.

Santa Claus who eats too much
  Is part of man's creation
Fantasies to please the young
  Are held in strict probation.

10-19-08

CAPACITY

Storage room within the brain
  There's room for more and more
Hidden are a million thoughts
  That surface, to keep score.

From day one you add and learn
  Each day you add a little
Complicated is your brain
  Its thoughts don't have a middle.

Your cup gets filled from God above
  It's filled with all your needs
Learning more of what He does
  Will rid your life of weeds.

10-19-08

DOWN ! NOT OUT!!!!

Weary from discomfort
  Sustained some vital blows
Need calming with compassion
  That led up to your woes.

When in life, this should occur
  The Lord is standing by
To heal your hurt and discomfort
  Allowing you to cry.

Avoiding seems not possible
  Unless you know His word
Remedies in the Bible
  Resolve all things, when heard.

Prayer and trust, the formula
  Is what is recommended
Understanding, hurts you feel
  His love and grace, is rendered.

10-19-08

AUTHORITY

Who's in charge, gives final say
  What will and will not be
Responsible for what takes place
  Has controlled authority.

Included are so many things
  That would fit the bill
Authority from the one in charge
  For oil— its, OK to drill.

Oil, food, planes and such
  Along with communication
Authorities make all the rules
  Throughout our great big nation.

When it comes to final authority
  God will take first place
In everything that you could name
  He is that winner of each race

10-19-08

DESTINY

Depending on the will of God
  What will the future be?
Uncertain, just what will take place
  This thing, called destiny.

All the things that change our life
  They could be big or small
How it made your chosen path
  I'm sure you can recall.

Destiny continues all through life
  Until the day you die
The future, controlled by God above
  His reasoning says—why?

10-19-08

SUCCESS

Achievements come in many forms
  Hard work will bring success
Focus on just one of those
  And give it all your best.

It might be wealth, it could be sports
  What ever you may chose
To get success, in what you pick
  Means effort, not to lose.

Success is yours, if healthy
  It has simple rules to win
Follow Jesus and have faith in God
  Much prayer, that you'll get in.

10-10-08

CONNECTION

Father and son, are closely knit
  They come in second to mother
Family ties, throughout the earth
  There're made much like each other.

Pedigree of animals
  Are kept within the realm
Special care when breeding
  Their owner, at the helm.

Cost is high, to accomplish this
  It's certified in writing
One day declared a winner
  Could be this exciting.

God creator, of all things
  His Son, He gave to save
Jesus filled, that needed void
  The heavenly road He paved.

10-10-08

ENCHANTED

Enchanted by His promises
  What waits for you and me
The beauty of His heaven
  Is what we long to see.

Our stay will be forever
  With no objects to keep time
No pills, or pain, or sickness
  A place where you'll feel fine.

Room for all His followers
  No work or bills to pay
Enjoy His golden mansions
  With lots of time to pray.

Imagination does run wild
  For this we pray and wait
When it's time to leave this world
  His call is never late.

10-12-08

MARRIAGE

Strangers making promises
  Are joined, as man and wife
Witnessed, before almighty God
  Now known as one, in life.

Chemistry of emotions
  Plays a vital part
Give and take, throughout their life
  Becomes a tactful art.

Bearing fruit, called children
  Once two, plus one, are three
Leaning on the Lord in prayer
  Could make life's trouble flee.

Modern age, has attitudes
  Confused, and full of fear
How this should be handled
  The Bible makes it clear.

10-15-08

HOLLYWOOD

Hollywood, the breeding place
  Of famous movie stars
A constant flow of talent
  Like genies, out of jars.

There are so many famous ones
  In times of long ago
Brought to life, on T.V. shows
  Are some I'm sure you know.

Classified as characters
  Some play horror scenes
Karloff and Lugosi
  Would make you hide, and scream.

Gangsters and the bad guys
  Were played by Cagney and Bogart
Edward G. fits this bill
  Their talent was an art.

Jimmy, Humphrey and Robinson
  Will stand out in your mind
Known for how they played their part
  Left others far behind.

Desperate to keep interest
  Much language and violence used
Animated characters and comedy

Thrown in, to keep who watched, amused.

Vivid tales, are brought to life
  Leave no imagination
No holes barred, in what takes place
  In the uncertain generation.

10-13-08

PYRAMIDS

A feat of unknown building
  Remains a mystery
How big stones, placed at great heights
  Still stand for all to see.

How big stones acquired
  Reached their place of use
Many slaves that labored
  Were victims of abuse.

Kings of old, built pyramids
  In time, would be their tomb
Hid inside this structure
  A special burial room.

Gold and all their valuables
  Placed close by their sides
In a casket made of gold
  Found their remains, still mummified.

10-11-08

PRIMITIVE MAN

Using things available
  Meant writing on the wall
Facts of all things taking place
  Used someday to recall.

Pictures, words and markings
  Each scene a different kind.
Primitive weapons, to protect and hunt
  With survival, on his mind.

Estimates how long ago
  Recorded as B.C.
Dinosaurs, that are extinct
  Made little creatures flee.

Safe inside caves where he lived
  Was replaced at early age
Strength determined, who was boss
  Some times with violent rage.

To reach the stage of modern man
  God stepped in with Christ the Lord
He paid in full, all debts we owed
  His will, we can afford.

10-13-08

119

CREATION

From the word God made all things
  And like Himself, made flesh
Night and day, and living things
  All wholesome new and fresh.

Once a favorite, now cast out
  The Devil sought his power
Satan uses all his tricks
  Weak souls, he will devour.

Use God's word to fight his foe
  It works good every time
Bible truths will stop his threats
  It did for yours and mine.

10-11-08

EMPHASIZE

Underlined, or printed red
  Made to stand out from the rest
This is done on lots of print
  To make sure you know what's best.

Emphasize, is what it's called
  Most Bibles do this well
Red letters, sometimes paragraphs
  To make all readers dwell.

Capital letters do the same
  They stand out from the rest
Instructions do this quite a bit
  When first using, you will test.

Embedded in your memory
  Many things that were emphasized
Some outstanding phrases
  Are good, when memorized.

10-8-08

MOTHER NATURE

Mother Nature is controlled by God
  He's Father of all things
Sometimes violent, sometimes good
  Is what this message brings.

Mother Nature, gets all the credit
  For happenings near and far
Yet she remains invisible
  Most times she's up to par.

Involved in all life's functions
  Her actions head the list
If we did not have her
  I am sure she would be missed.

10-8-08

THROUGH THE YEARS

The many trials He put you through
  Needed steps to qualify
A product of the spoken word
  On God, you still rely.

Life had its doubting moments
  Although your faith was strong
Many sins you had forgiven
  When you admitted you did wrong.

Do not boast, how good you have been
  Be humble, His request
Reflect His love and teachings
  Until you are His guest.

10-7-08

TEMPTATION

Out of view, out of mind
  Could these become relation?
What you see, is what you want
  This leads into temptation.

Fantasies within the brain
  Mixed in with what we see
Imagination could run wild
  Out of ten, you might reach three.

Satan has a list that's long
  He'll put them on display
There are so many tricks he plays
  If fooled, you'll have his way.

When you're tempted, don't think twice
  You've given him the edge
The slightest opening, is all he needs
  He'll make use of his destructive wedge

10-7-08

ORIGINAL

One of a kind, declared original
　Increase in value every day
Some are famous paintings
　Or baked objects, made of clay.

Duplicates of originals
　Are sometimes hard to tell
Asking price is high on those
　When it comes time to sell.

Our God made us original
　No two are just the same
Even twins are different
　Personalities, and their name.

God sent His Son, original
　In heaven, He doth dwell
His enemy, the Devil
　Resides way down in hell.

10-5-08

TRIBULATION AND OPPRESSION

Tribulation and oppression
  Most times, go hand in hand
Lack of most necessities
  Must make use each bit and strand.

Each time disaster happens
  Some left, are still alive
Help is sent from all around
  Will help victims to survive.

Earthquakes, floods and hurricanes
  Most times its path we know
When and where it's headed for
  And how fast the winds will blow.

Tornados are less predictable
  They're never out of season
Could form and strike most anywhere
  Conditions make the reason.

Highs and lows are everywhere
  Some sunshine or some rain
When variations are extreme
  Many people will complain.

10-5-08

1945 Greene Avenue, Brooklyn, NY. Left to Right:
father Frank, mother Margaret, sister Louise and me.

TEMPERATURE

The atmosphere we live in
  Is filled with hot and cold
Our food is now refrigerated
  So it don't rot or mold.

So many things affected
  At times, it's hard to reason
Why some like heat, all the time
  The rest want change of season.

Folks live near the equator
  They thrive and like it well
Eskimos in igloos
  They build, and in them dwell.

Seems that God has favored
  The Northern Hemisphere
Where Christ was born, and spent His life
  Along with others here.

Hot or cold, but not luke warm
  He wants your interest HOT
Knowing all about the Lord, takes time
  You walk, before you trot.

10-3-08

SUN AND RAIN

Fading rays of sunshine
  As it sets out in the west
Silhouettes at twilight time
  Are seen before we rest.

Rainy days don't have this joy
  There is no sun to set
Water needed for all things that grow
  We'll dry when we get wet.

Sun and rain are needed
  To grow things in their field
Without both, our crops would die
  And nothing, they will yield.

All of Gods creation, not just only man
  Depend on both of these
From the smallest blade of grass
  To the giant Redwood trees.

10-2-08

THREE STRIKES

Three strikes, your OUT, you had a chance
  You failed this many times
Incarcerate , throw away the key
  You're not deterred by fines.

The umpire, now becomes the judge
  Your record shows the score
Lessons learned, from all things past
  Forgot when you sinned more.

There's no excuse for angry flares
  Of happenings in the past
Emotions, made you act like this
  It seems they'll always last.

Hardened in the ways of hell
  The Devil has no soul
This could be the reason why
  Your actions you can't control.

10-4-08

BOTTOM LINE

All things that we total
  To get a bottom line
There are so many choices
  They are things of your design.

Confronted with each day we face
  The list is very long
Plus or minus, what comes next
  Your actions must belong.

At times we can't make up our mind
  Deciding what to do
Options fill a wondering mind
  There are more, than just a few.

Asking God to help decide
  Prayer needed, for this direction
Assured by Him, your choice is right
  Another bottom line connection.

10-4-08

SYMPATHETIC

Sympathetic tears are shed
  Sad emotions bring this on
Many things could trigger this
  Like friends, when they are gone.

Be thankful you're not the victim
  Now you share another pain
Their morning loss, of loved ones
  You made your feelings plain.

Those who saw Lord Jesus die
  Shed tears of sympathy
Thinking that it was the end
  When He deceased upon that tree.

Surprised when God restored His life
  He convinced each doubting Thomas
Jesus washed us clean with blood He shed
  And fulfilled His utmost promise.

10-3-08

LET THEM KNOW

Get it over, do it quick
  Have other things in mind
That's the way some people act
  Somewhere, sometime you'll find.

Lose focus of what's taken place
  Can't seem to just fit in
All keyed up, in self desires
  Their loss is not your win.

An understanding, loving heart
  Will answer, with forgiveness
Future happenings of this kind
  Should be labeled strictly business.

This could be a loved one
  Or someone you admire
They don't know they have this fault
  Unless you light their fire.

AMBITION

Full of pep and vigor
  Ambition to make a gain
Efforts to accomplish this
  You are now put under strain.

Ideas that form within your mind
  Will soon become desire
Sorting out how this can be
  Soon sets your mind on fire

Crazy folks can play mean jokes
  They live from day to day
Just use their brain for simple things
  The lack shows some decay.

Keep active with ambition
  Until they day you die
It could be the only thing you take
  To Heaven in the sky.

SUFFICIENT

Not to little, not to much
  It's just the right amount
Most everything that we call waste
  Could fill a needy account.

Over eating, more than sufficient
  Obesity is in store
Life cut short, because of this
  All warnings, they ignore.

Sufficient says you have enough
  No need for great excess
Just enough to fill your needs
  For this, you'll have to guess.

NOT THAT OLD

The spirit young, the body old
  Most things are still intact
No back flips, or unsafe things
  It's time you act your age.

Experience and wisdom
  The brain is full of these
Let others know, you still think sharp
  GA SUND HEIT when they sneeze.

You may recall each spring and fall
  The things you did outside
Good times were spent to fish and hunt
  And enjoy the countryside.

I still enjoy the beauty
  Of all the things I see
Watch others work, while I just watch
  I'm retired now and free.

9-30-08

EXPECTATIONS

The wind makes troubled waters
  With waves at sea, that are high
The oncoming storm, will soon be here
  With great lightning and darkened sky.

In magnitude, some times we face
  Such a violation blow
We pray to God we will survive
  And much safety He will bestow.

When it's calm, we should not forget
  And pray with gratitude
Don't wait for another tragedy
  To put you in this mood.

Luxury and infinity
  Is what your new home awaits
Enjoyment 'cause there are no storms
  Behind Heaven's pearly gates.

10-2-08

INDISPENSABLE

When calculating things we need
  We make a list that's sensible
The most important tops the list
  Because they're considered indispensable.

People who have talent
  That no one else can match
Indispensable for the things they do
  And are very hard to catch.

Jesus Christ is just like that
  His miracles make Him so
Indispensable, one of a kind
  That all the world should know.

God made Him indispensable
  With hopes we act like Him
His mission was to make us clean
  And free us from all sin.

9-29-08

SUSPENSE

A build up of emotion
  Not knowing what comes next
Writers wrote just that way
  It's found within the text.

The Bible is filled with stories
  Happening of all kinds
Tales of situations
  There are many that one finds.

Sins today are just like those
  That happened long ago
Details are mentioned thoroughly
  To make sure that you know.

When in doubt you're sure to find
  The problem on your mind
Somewhere in its pages
  The answers you will find.

10-1-08

GOLDEN YEARS

Twilight time or golden years
  With age you fit this term
A life fulfilled with ups and downs
  For heaven now, you yearn.

Golden years have many things
  You did not have when young
"Praise the Lord" you lived this long
  To see what has been done.

Proud to be called grandpa or ma
  Enjoy how they perform
A bright new generation
  That keeps our country strong.

This cycle keeps on going
  Until our Lord returns
The world we know, will be free from sin
  Sing praise, as the Devil burns.

9-28-08

ALL SAINTS DAY

November first, is All Saints Day
  That follows Halloween
Gone, are all the gory ones
  With the trick or treaters seen.

Those, who excel in Godly things
  Most likely make the list
God selects his chosen few
  That others might have missed.

Dedication and good works
  Most likely lead the way
Now you could be celebrated
  That others might have missed that day.

9-28-08

GOLD AND HONEY

When precious metals are spoken of
  Most times it will be gold
Long before our Lord appeared
  It was said in stories told.

Sweetness, known in ancient times
  Honey would top them all
Heaven is filled with both of these
  And makes our world look small.

Gold will shine forever
  Like our precious Lord above
Honey can't match His sweetness
  Or his gracious gift of love.

These two items that are mentioned
  Are proven quality
Heaven is filled with both of these
  They wait for you and me.

9-28-08

CHEERS

Cheers have been the standards
  With tributes and applause
Tradition keeps this system
  For every worthy cause.

You might hear 'Hip Hip Hooray'
  Along with great ovation
That's the way we celebrate
  Great things throughout our nation.

Football games and baseball games
  Are filled with lots of cheers
Times when favorite teams will score
  I cover both of my ears.

Cheering helps to stimulate
  And makes the team excel
Sharpen up your vocal cords
  Many cheers you soon will yell.

9-28-08

IMPRESSIVE

Impressive is a quality
  That ranks high above the rest
Like God with all His majesty
  It's nothing but the best.

Keeping tabs on followers
  Forgiving all their sins
Overjoyed with happiness
  With each new soul He wins.

Many words can't say enough
  Now He impresses us
No limit to His love and grace
  He starts by saying thus.

When you seek to be impressed
  Look for that knowing nod
Impressed throughout their lifetime
  By an impressive loving God.

9-28-08

BEATITUDES

The Beatitudes are meant for everyone
  Who might feel the overwhelm
Making clear uncertainties
  Taught by Jesus at the helm.

Many things that man might face
  The list has ten in all
Blessed, you are called by Him
  Advised, so you don't fall.

Followers of the Christian faith
  Confronted with these things
Blessed, are the ears that hear
  The teaching Jesus brings.

The blessed life in Matthew 5
  Describe in much detail
Knowing that the flesh is weak
  Are there so you don't fail.

9-28-08

GOOD ADVICE

The Devil is an expert, at every kind of sin
  He's waiting and egar to show you how
He'll make big, all our sins called small
  With hopes you will allow.

Unexpected methods
  To make you play his game
Once you're trapped within his web
  That's where you will remain.

Be aware, the Bible says
  Put on the coat of armor
Don't be fooled by promises
  From that lying evil charmer.

God knows how he operates
  His word, your best defense
To ward off Satan every time
  God's advice still makes good sense.

10-26-08

RICH OR POOR

When it comes to money
  You might be rich or poor
Most of us are in between
  We'll stay that way for sure.

People, just like snow flakes
  God made us not the same
Different features and abilities
  Some limp considered lame.

Risen souls that live in heaven
  Are free from all these things
That's the way God handles this
  Eternal life, His promise brings.

Rich people still have needs
  The poor man just gets by
When deceased they're equal
  Take nothing when they die.

9-27-08

PRICES

Don't be fooled with big letters
  Read all the print that's small
Advertisement does this thing
  With hopes, to make you fall.

Reduced postage on the envelope
  Could be another clue
Thousands of lucky winners have won
  Not just only you.

Sometimes you'll get a bargain
  The offer is 'LA-GIT'
Competition, makes the price come down
  RESULTS—— a small profit.

Big companies charge a higher price
  Pay more, for what you get
Reputations of transactions past
  Many people don't forget.

9-27-08

WAN-A-BE

When you idolize professionals
A famous movie star, you'd like to be
Your name in lights or the hall of fame
But you're just A-WAN-A-BE.

Dreams are made of things like this
They set your mind on fire
Unrelated happenings
You become what you desire.

Reality don't work that quick
Although you're fancy free
Special efforts on your part
Says you're still A-WAN-A-BE.

9-27-08

PETITIONED PRAYER

A single prayer to God himself
　To make good a bad condition
When many pray the same request
　Appeals are now a petition.

Constant prayer to make a change
　We pray to get attention
His love and grace, is what we ask
　With hope for intervention.

Only by His love for us
　May miracles take place
Ask those who are examples
　Of His overflowing grace.

9-24-08

FALL

September is here, summer is gone
  Pumpkins are now in style
Jack Frost is waiting patiently
  For the winter time to smile.

Halloween, soon will be here
  Observed in many places
Trick or treat with hands held out
  Kids dressed with funny faces.

Thanking God at harvest time
  For things that grew well
Thanksgiving time is next in line
  Roast turkey you can smell.

Moving on, the pace is quick
  Since Christmas time is near
Swearing in our new president
  As we start another year.

9-25-08

1947: My first car – a 1923 Plymouth. I bought and sold it for $125.00. It had a habit of losing its wheels. This picture was taken in front of the clubhouse that we rented. From left to right: Harry Carmerson, unknown, Pete McLoughin, Harold Mahlstedt, Harold Gartner.

INVITATION

When you are invited
  And join others for an event
It ends the same with RSVP
  On all invitations sent.

Consider it a privilege
  That you were asked to come
Unexpected invitations will surprise you
  And tell you who it's from

Those who know the Lord and God
  Don't need an invitation
Bible quotes will tell you this
  From inspired inspiration.

It's not a club, but it's a group
  Who learned things from the Word
Get involved with God and Son
  Since first the Word was heard.

9-24-08

PETTY

Small compared to what is huge
  You might say it is petty
Don't be fooled because of size
  He's waiting if you're ready.

Satan tries all avenues
  He's deceiving, mean, and strong
Sway his way a little bit
  He wants you to belong.

Although considered petty
  Sin grows without God's help
God knows how to deal with him
  When he hits below the belt.

Keep in mind he's always there
  If you should drop your guard
Consider him not petty
  And stay out of his yard.

9-22-08

HABITS

Habits formed in early years
  Are difficult to break
Changes are the way to go
  A different road you'll take.

Tactics must be fortified
  With prayer and consideration
God will help you take control
  If Jesus Christ you mention.

Redeeming power is put in place
  The Lord will help your cause
When you're free and clear again
  Joy is truly yours.

9-22-08

SATISFACTION

Satisfaction guaranteed
　You have thirty days to try
This printed plain upon the box
　Of most things that you buy.

It should work well and fill your needs
　No risk they say you'll take
Substitutes some times you'll get
　This offer sometimes a fake.

Most companies try to please
　With hopes that you'll buy more
They discount things they have to sell
　Much less than any store.

Quality and good price
　Will beat the competition
Find all the things you'll ever need
　For hunting and good fishing.

Reputation, speed, and honesty
　For quality you'll pay more
Satisfied with many things
　You bought there once before.

9-23-08

MEMBERS

Membership cards are issued
  Your name says you belong
When you give donations
  They sing the same old song.

Since you are a member
  A yearly fee required
If you give more than they ask
  You're flattered and admired.

Membership that has no cards
  It also has no dues
Learn what it is all about
  It's printed in "Good News."

Help from other members
  Will share what you should know
When you are a member
  To heaven you will go.

9-22-08

RECIPES

A blended list of what goes in
  Will please all those who taste
An appetizing thing to eat
  That is sure to have no waste.

A little of this and a little of that
  Once made from memory
Now it comes out just the same
  Since it become a recipe.

A list of all ingredients
  That go into a mix
A way to blend them will take place
  A tasty dish you'll fix.

Cookbooks filled with recipes
  Are tried and proven dishes
How to make all kinds of food
  And tasty little fishes.

Specialties are there in print
  Just waiting to be tried
Many chefs from round the world
  Reveal what others hide.

9-22-08

ACCEPT

Accept your situation
  With disposition great
All good things will happen
  To faithful ones who wait.

Anticipate and don't give in
  With grace our God decides
His followers are chosen ones
  He keeps them and provides.

Don't be anxious, don't lose faith
  When ready He'll bestow
Many things you don't expect
  That will make your spirit grow.

Humility and faith in God
  A desired bottom line
Walk daily with his Son the Lord
  The outcome will be fine.

9-22-08

GOSPEL TRAIN

It's Sunday, first day of the week
  In church, one hour is spent
The GOSPEL TRAIN is here again
  On time for this event.

A pastor reads the Bible
  To all the congregation
This takes place at 11 am
  Elsewhere throughout our nation.

A chosen sermon, from the Word
  Some others will remain
Next Sunday he will preach again
  And conduct the gospel train.

9-22-08

DEATH AND TAXES

When you're alive there are two things
  From which there is no escape
Death and taxes are those things
  Put first while others wait.

IRS says give it up
  No excuses for why not
If you falsify or cheat
  In prison you will rot.

Death will put an end to this
  And stop the tax each year
Relatives will spend what's left
  At last you're free and clear.

9-21-08

FAIRY TALES

Tweedle Dee and Tweedle Dum
Fictitious and discreet
Dee don't know where Dum is
He roams with two left feet.

Both reside in fairy tales
Like mermaids and pink whales
Imaginary Characters
Shapely girls, with fish like tails.

Don't know if they're in Disney land
Along with Tinker Bell
They might be hidden somewhere
Should come out if loud you yell.

When you go to sleep at night
They might be in your dreams
You will know they're present
One sings, the other screams.

9-21-08

GOOD ADVICE

Put on hold, is what you 're told
  Are things you need refrained
Sodium will be head of the list
  Must rid those pounds you gained.

Eat good things and exercise
  No hamburgers from the griddle
Keep in shape with this advice
  Avoid that great big middle.

Smoking will cause problems
  That leads to many things
A habit, that is hard to break
  In print – a warning brings.

Once thought cool, is now taboo
  Statistics tell you why
They discourage you , by price increased
  With hopes, you will not buy.

9-21-08

COMPETITION

When you enter tournaments
  And you expect to win
Out think , out smart opponents
  And make their chances slim.

Don't under estimate competitors
  They might be very good
Let others know you're here to win
  Make your winning understood.

Specialize, and do your best
  Don't try to do them all
Keep in place, a safety net
  Just in case you fall.

Winning is not everything
  The joy is being there
Win or lose it is p to you
  Your talent you can share.

9-20-08

VOCABULARY

A chosen variety of spoken words
  Describe what you present
Put in such a fashion
  With much time and effort spent.

Try to fit a word that rhymes
  Requires much deep thought
Not like on some T.V. shows
  Where missing vowels are brought.

Make the change and rearrange
  The words that sound the same
The challenge of this action
  Soon becomes a game.

Dictionaries sure do help
  To increase the words you use
Catchy lines might do the trick
  Depending what you choose.

9-18-08

BEING UNDERSTOOD

Messages that have no words
  Made some times with sad eyes
Could be things that you approve
  Or things that you despise.

Body language is the same
  Conveying thoughts of mind
Expressions put together
  You may be cross or kind?

How you act and what you do
  Don't require words you speak
Like the eyes and body
  When done, —called "Tongue In Cheek"

When this takes place, you're sure to know
  How other people feel
Making sure that you're understood
  This vocal is ideal!!!

9-19-08

LIFE'S ROUTINE

When work is done, and daylight fades
   And the sun sinks low out west
Feed your face, kick off your shoes
   Watch T.V., relax, sit down and rest.

This might sound familiar
   A routine takes place each day
Weekends are quite different
   On Saturday we recreate, come Sunday - church and
pray.

Vacation time comes in between
   You can visit or stay home
Finish what you started
   Or relax and just lie prone.

Do this until you're 65
   It's then you can retire
Do what ever makes your day
   Spend time of your desire.

9-19-08

ANTICIPATION

Looking forward to a great event
  You're anxious and can hardly wait
You're built up in anticipation
  For what takes place this date.

Weddings, newborns, head the list
  Birthdays, Christmas, next in turn
Anticipation of these too come
  With patience you will yearn.

Must fill your mind with other things
  That makes time evaporate
Anticipation will soon slow down
  And ease the time you wait.

Waiting time you're sure to know
  No matter where you go
When you're in a hurry
  Anticipation makes it slow.

9-20-08

COMPROMISE

I'll give an inch, if you give one
  But please don't take a mile
We'll come up with a bottom line
  Then both of us will smile.

It don't matter what takes place
  There's different points of view
Seems there are so many
  I can only list a few.

Politics is on the list
  Sling mud so they can win
Another topic to avoid
  Most likely is religion.

Debating gives the reason why
  You feel the way you do
Budgets need compromise
  When buying something new.

9-19-08

WEARY

Weary from what took place, till now
  And all your energy is spent
Frustration, along with lots of work
  Can make sleep the big event.

Eyes are drooped, exclaim you're pooped
  Exhausted, spent and tired
Wound up in this condition 'cause
  You did all the things desired.

Don't matter if you're young or old
  At times, you will get weary
Take time out and get some rest
  On days, considered dreary.

Being weary, don't last long
  It's part of how we live
Most likely this happen
  Only when your up most,—give.

9-20-08

170

MEMORIES

Embracing fond, the memories
  That took place, long ago
Seems like only yesterday
  The things that made us glow.

Recalling all the pleasant thoughts
  The list could be quite long
Put aside the not-so-goods
  When everything went wrong.

Give and take, what lies ahead
  You'll find out what's in store
God's grace will take care of all things
  In ways that are galore.

When you Stop and reminisce
  Recalling what took place
Keep in mind positives
  With smiles upon your face.

9-17-08

TRIVIA

Trivia is so many things
  If you recall the facts they ask
The answer, you will hope to know
  Revealed now in your task.

The many things that did take place
  Great numbers I recall
Depending on the categories
  No one can know them all.

If you play the game a lot
  Much info you'll acquire
Who invented many things
  And what started the Chicago fire.

In your brain is stored the facts
  To your lips you must transfer
When your memory does recall
  Pops-up the needed answer.

9-17-08

OVER THE HILL

"Over the hill" they call us
  Because our youth has flown
We still do all things slower
  At times, we grunt and groan.

In time the youth will get this way
  You're sure to hear them shout
Just because we're up in age
  Don't mean our fire is out.

Youth don't last forever
  It fades with " Father Time"
Staying young don't last that long
  That you can call your prime.

If you're endowed and still have health
  " Over the hill " you don't belong
Act young, have faith and remember
  It was God who made you strong.

9-18-08

HAGGLE

Don't expect the asking price
  From those who want to buy
Most likely they will haggle
  After giving it a try.

When you're shopping in the market
  You'll most likely do the same
Buy or sell what's second hand
  You learn to play this game.

Once was new, it served you well
  Good function still is there
It should last for quite sometime
  Cause it was given up most care.

Products on the market
  Quickly will be sold
When the price is justified
  No haggling will unfold.

9-14-08

MAGNITUDE

Mother nature's devastating storms
  Each season they will come
In magnitude they're measured
  And where they're headed from.

Some are weak and don't destroy
  While others tear things down
Tornados cut an ugly path
  That flatten most of town.

Earthquakes score in magnitude
  Depending on the shift
Living where this don't take place
  You could say it is quite a gift.

Seismographs and weathermen
  Will keep us in the know
Recorded was the magnitude
  How violet was the blow.

8-30-08

HANDYMAN

Looking through the classifieds
  Are ads, when they are ran
They look for Mr. Fix it
  It reads wanted, HANDY MAN.

Leaky faucets, doors don't shut
  Could be most any thing
Tighten all loose handles
  And fix bells that do not ring.

When you make things work again
  And wages are fair price
Now you and boss are satisfied
  Because you did things nice.

8-23-08

PROPHECY

Prophecy has in store
  What the future holds
Predicting all the happenings
  Before the act unfolds.

Details, some times, are left out
  The rest, could all come true
What takes place, all will find out
  Not only me and you.

God let prophets tell their tales
  To them, He made it known
The gift, He gave to just a few
  Directly from His throne.

8-29-08

DIFFER

Agreeing is a positive
  All negatives will differ
Positives want all things strong
  They seem to like things stiffer.

When you have all things your way
  Many times, your choice is wrong
Give and take, and rearrange
  Put things where they belong.

Agreeing helps, to make it right
  Debating gets it solved
Different strokes, for different folks
  Satisfaction now resolved.

8-29-08

MEDDLING

Meddling could be a thing
  That people do not like
Don't moderate, and don't butt in
  They'll say "go take a hike."

It's not meant for you to know
  They don't want your opinion
Mind your business, and retreat
  Remain in your dominion.

Your meddling is still not wanted
  They're still looking for a cure
Doing this makes matters worse
  This notice is for sure.

8-30-08

ACCUMULATE

STOP! Just look around
  At things you once thought funny
If you did not have these things
  You'd have a pile of money.

A garage sale might be just the thing
  Cause there's no room for more
I am sure you'll find replacements
  While shopping at the store.

When you accumulate another pile
  Procedure is the same
Now you have more room again
  What's left, will still remain.

8-31-08

GOOD NEWS

Good news is always welcome
  Most headlines favor bad
Many things that go to print
  Are bound to make you sad.

Sports, events, and comics
  Are what you'll find inside
Prediction of the weather
  And when we'll have high tide.

New Testament is called "Good News"
  Records what Jesus did
From the time that he was born
  And when he was a kid.

Spread the joy, it is Good News
  The promise does unfold
The babe, who came at Christmas time
  And was born out in the cold.

8-30-08

HOARDING

Accumulate more than you use
  And hoard more than you need
There are some who act like this
  And do it for the greed.

At time there's barely just enough
  To fill the needs of others
Greedy people that hoard things
  Is what this message covers.

Get only things you can consume
  Even though it's free
Share the products others use
  Now happy they will be.

8-30-08

182

TWILIGHT

It's not light, and not quite dark
  Soon stars will brightly shine
This happens dawn and evening
  It's known as twilight time.

When the sun sets in the west
  It's light for quite awhile
Darkness comes, from clouds and rain
  Because it is their style.

Animals will show their face
  And come out of the brush
Not often is it trophy time
  Same as a royal flush.

8-31-08

FLATTER

Compliments are welcome words
  To some they really matter
You can store up brownie points
  With the ones you flatter.

Flattering can open doors
  That are most times shut
You could lift the ego
  Of someone in a rut.

Do not overdo all the things you say
  Keep conversation nice
Save some thoughts for other times
  And put the rest on ice.

8-31-08

BANQUET

A banquet is a party
  It could be called a feast
Get together for some fun
  Let all your troubles cease.

It may follow meetings
  That take place now and then
Set a time for all who come
  Say when we'll meet again.

Stuff your face with lots of food
  Delicious it will be
Take your pick in what you like
  And don't eat all you see.

Limit what there is to eat
  That means, don't fill your plate
It will happen, come next year
  Until then, you wait.

8-30-08

BETTER

Better is the next step up
  From the bottom you must start
Two steps up, and one step back
  You're gaining, says the chart.

Persistent be, in time you'll see
  Your effort made things better
If you win the race you run
  You might receive a letter.

Eliminate what can go wrong
  And be a strong GO GETTER
Enjoy whatever you like best
  Now that you're doing better.

8-31-08

186

WAITING

Waiting can be all you do
  If patient, that you are
Seems no matter where you go
  It could be near or far.

Be on time, and don't be late
  Appointments that you make
Hurry, just to get there
  Then waiting time, you'll take.

They're always on the minus side
  Even when there's cancellation
It be awhile 'til you get called
  Since you reached your destination.

8-28-08

BLEMISHES

Blemishes are hidden scars
  Not meant for eyes to see
Wounds that heal, you might conceal
  So more appeal might be.

Products that have blemishes
  In price they are reduced
All things else, will still work fine
  No need that it be spruced.

Could be a scratch, perhaps a dent
  And still it is brand new
Look around, perhaps you'll find
  I'm sure they have a few.

8-28-08

INTROVERT OR EXTROVERT

Bold and loud or soft and shy
  Are people that you see
Extrovert or Introvert
  It could be you or me.

Somewhere in your growing up
  You were loud or shy
How you dealt with those around
  Might be the reason why.

Emotions are built in your genes
  They play the biggest part
Some could be most brilliant
  Or have the gift of art.

All through life you'll stay the same
  Can't change your category
You will remain, most bold or shy
  And repeat the same old story.

9-2-08

ACCEPT

When you approve, and do accept
  The final bottom line
Knowing all the details
  All things should turn out fine.

When you change, or disagree
  What other people think
Untangle thoughts, and smooth things out
  Removing every kink.

Secret info is locked up
  A few know where it's kept
When exposed, to all concerned
  They accept it, or reject.

9-2-08

DESCRIBE

Description is what you convey
  The object you describe
Could be something simple
  Or a far-off ancient tribe.

How you go about your thoughts
  Depends on many things
Why the topic came to mind
  And what the message brings.

Some things really test your mind
  To what you must recall
Calculate and concentrate
  It requires all your all.

9-2-08

APPETITE

Satisfying all your needs
  Until you feel just right
Could be food or knowledge
  A thing called appetite.

Eating 'til your stomach's full
  Is a longing in the brain
There's just so many you can chose
  For now, some must remain.

When you find the thing you sought
  You're ready for another
Keep eyes peeled, and look around
  In time, you will discover.

9-2-08

SELDOM VS. FREQUENT

The opposite of frequent
  Is seldom, which means "not very much"
When you don't communicate
  You'll soon be out of touch.

Human nature has a way
  To refrain from many things
Seldom are your dreams fulfilled
  Of what your memory brings.

Smoking, could be seldom
  They say "Do not inhale"
When you do you will create
  Another coffin nail.

Frequently, I try to write
  Whatever comes to mind
All the words that surface
  At times are hard to find.

9-2-08

BELONGING

When you are a member
  You're conformed, and sing their song
Now your name is on their list
  It says that you belong.

Could be a church, or special group
  A political organization
Single out what you like best
  There are many throughout the nation.

When you join a group that's new
  You are a charter member
When you're asked for dates and such
  I'm sure that you'll remember.

Meetings, plans, and things to come
  Are put on the agenda
You'll have a say in what takes place
  A service that you render.

9-2-08

ABOLISH

Get rid of, and abolish
  All the things you've grown to hate
Priority will head the list
  While those in turn, must wait.

Eliminate what irritates
  What things that you deem wrong
Find the way to accomplish this
  Then sing a happy song.

Abolish things that fit this phase
  That put you in a stew
How you abolish, what goes or stays
  I'll leave that up to you.

9-2-08

COMMOTION

Ambulance and fire trucks enroute
  Create excitement and commotion
Shatters all the silence
  And stirs up your locomotion.

Peace and quiet are disturbed
  With all the noise they make
Just look inside your oven
  Now fallen is your cake.

Bells and sirens ring quite loud
  It might make people nervous
Not often does this happen
  It comes along with service.

9-2-08

DECEPTION

Deception comes in many forms
  The Devil knows them all
How he used it many times
  I know you will recall.

His policy is dishonesty
  He is good at what he does
He fooled so many people
  When he filled their blipps and blurs.

GOD allows this evil one
  The action, to deceive
We are saved and never fooled
  'Cause CHRIST made us believe.

One day soon, I pray it's quick
  He'll be removed forever
No more will he deceive mankind
  In ways that were most clever.

9-2-08

FREIGHT

Freight is loaded on a train
  Trucks bring it to your door
Delivered food is also freight
There's always room for more.

Sometimes there might be damage
  From handling wind or rain
When you don't like its condition
  You let them know, when you complain.

Parcels big, are known as freight
  While some of them are small
If you have the ways and means
  The product you can haul.

Transportation needed
  For so many things
Even letters from afar
  Are freight the mailman brings.

Made in far-off places
  They ship it everywhere
Most likely made in CHINA
  'Cause labor is cheaper there.

9-6-08

MURPHY'S LAW

When disaster follows jeopardy
  Many problems are in store
Results are yours, if you're involved
  They call it *Murphy's Law.*

Piled up, a mound of things gone wrong
  A list from A to Z
It happens to the best of us
  It could be you or me?

Pick out any subject
  I'm sure it will go wrong
There is no happy ending
  You'll sing a loser's song.

Take my advice and steer clear
  Away from *Murphy's Law*
You'll score, when things are positive
  When Murphy, you ignore.

9-7-08

TINKER

Tinker with most everything
  The challenge, you desired
The need to fix, when things are broke
  A talent you've acquired.

Don't be confused with Tinkerbell
  Who lives in Disneyland
She only lives in fairy tales
  And has a magic wand in hand.

Sometimes tools are needed
  To make it work once more
Could save you lots of money
  If new, bought at the store.

There are so many things that break
  You're tested every time
Tinker 'til it works once more
  What's fixed is yours or mine.

9-6-08

RETIRED

When you're employed, you have a job
  To fill the bosses' needs
You get paid a salary
  For your skills and deeds.

40 hours, most time spent
  You're paid a given rate
Taken out are tax and such
  Deductions, when you're late.

Comes the time there is no need
  The boss replies "YOU'RE FIRED."
When you stay 'til 65
  You then become, RETIRED.

9-7-08

My wife Martha, age 20. This picture was taken in
front of the Mellenger's at Oliver Lake in La Grange,
Indiana. Our first date was at the roller rink.

SERVICE

Many things to fill your needs
  For service you might pay
Skilled personnel to do the job
  Might need them, come the day.

Service also comes from GOD
  His grace you'll always need
Christ is there to set things right
  A service great — INDEED!

9-6-08

ANIMALS AND PETS

Domesticated animals
  Are fed and kept inside
Made to know you're friendly
  They stay close by your side.

Beware of untamed animals
  That once lived in the wild
Could injure you at any time
  "Cause that's the way they're styled.

If you get them while they're young
  They'll treat you with respect
Grownups still have instincts
  Attack, when you least suspect.

Take advice from those who know
  From experience, they were taught
Don't rely on what you think
  Give danger a second thought.

When you hear "LET WILD THINGS BE"
  It's a very sound advice
Get your pets from friends or stores
  You know they'll treat you nice.

9-6-08

GIFTS AND TREASURES

Many gifts and treasures
  Are stored in your abode
Things that you acquired
  While traveling on the road.

Memories you remember
  Of all your visits there
Items, that recall your trips
  At times, with people share.

GOD gave you many treasures
  Are things, you can not see.
Jesus Christ is one of them
  A gift you share with me.

Love and grace are on that list
  He put joy within your heart.
Another gift is friendship
  You'll keep 'til you depart.

9-4-08

ADVERTISED ITEMS

Items, just like people
  All have different names.
Help you to identify
  "Cause none are made the same.

Advertising tell you many things
  Because they want to sell.
How it changes all defects
  And how it makes you well.

If it works the way they say
  You're thankful for the luck.
Untrue, are some promises
  That made you spend your buck.

Be aware of what is said
  It could be another lie.
Second opinions always help
  In products that you buy.

9-7-08

KNOWLEDGE

Accumulated knowledge
  Could be worthwhile trend
Store it in your brain somewhere
  A thirst, that has not end.

Keep ready to learn something new
  For some, it might be old.
Added to the facts you know
  You're not left in the cold.

Everyone knows something
  You can add into your list.
Somewhere, somehow, along the way
  This knowledge you have missed.

Everyday, you have the chance
  To ask, and wonder why
This desire keeps on going
  Until the day you die.

9-7-08

VOLUNTEERS

Volunteers assemble
  To get things underway
Since there is not profit
  There isn't any pay.

Unpaid help is needed
  For so many things
Most times, to help a charity
  Is what this message brings.

When the cause will help mankind
  The need is understood
Volunteers will be on hand
  And make things turn out good.

Just because they're up in age
  Don't mean their need is through
Someday, in time, we'll reach that stage
  It will be ME AND YOU.

9-8-08

THING

UNATTACHED – the word called thing
  Sometimes referred as stuff
It fits so many places
  Most estimates are rough.

It satisfies the moment
  Until you do decide
What it's called, and how it's used
  You'll find out when it's tried.

Until they come up with a name
  It will remain, a thing
Looking for a catchy phrase
  The name that others bring.

9-9-08

IMPORTS

Most things we buy are imports
  At times, were made right here
Since then, big companies moved abroad
  'Cause labor is cheaper there.

Good quality is a must
  Reliable the same
Supervised by Americans
  And changed not, is its name.

China makes the biggest part
  Of all things that we use
Put their name on clothes you wear
  Most likely, on your shoes.

This system will get bigger
  In time, might even double
That's the sign of changing times
  Could be in for big trouble.

9-8-08

INVESTIGATE

Looking for a way to solve
  You look around and wait
Take on the role of Sherlock Holmes
  Get facts, and investigate.

Find all the whys and wherefors
  Look for clues that may be found
Clues that have revealings
  Are some time on the ground.

Put your finds together
  The answer should be clear
ELEMENTARY! States the Great One
  The word, that you might hear.

9-7-08

FAMILIARITY

Advice that's freely given
  Is meant for one and all
Could prevent great injury
  And keep you from a fall.

Familiarity breeds contempt
  When you're over confident
Hold on to what you know is safe
  The thought is time well spent.

Hold on to your trust in God
  He is your safety net
His grace provides protection
That you will not regret.

9-8-08

MASQUERADE

An expert at disguises
  I'm sure he knows them all
Masquerading is his game
  He's waiting if you fall.

He has the skill to fool you
  When your resilience hits a low
His evil hits your target
  It could be a fatal blow.

Hold on when danger is at hand
  Hold tight so you don't fall
The Devil hopes you'll lose your grip
  And wind up in his stall.

Pray to GOD, he'll give you strength
  And keep you from his sin
Nurtured by his love and grace
  Your battle scored a win.

9-8-08

MISCELLANEOUS

Discarded bits and pieces
  Of things that once were ours
Collections of so many things
  That filled up many jars.

Saved a bunch of nuts and bolts
  To fix things, if they broke
Even found some old ash trays
  Of days I used to smoke.

Lots of things, like safety pins
  Buttons by the score
Unmatched keys, and bobby pins
  Had room for more, and more.

Time to rid, what is now junk
  Reduce the mound in size
Bet you have, what I threw out
  Before you realized.

9-13-08

REDEEMED

Accumulate good deeds and such
  To get back what is good
That's what God has promised us
  He made that understood.

He sent His son, Lord Jesus
  To show us what he had in mind
Forgave us all our earthly faults
  So we were not left behind.

Was known as our redeemer
  Who washed away our sin
Paid our debts with blood he shed
  Made Satan's chances slim.

Made known, what GOD had promised
  No coupons to redeem
Now we're free from Satan's hold
  Like snow, he washed us clean.

9-13-08

TODAY'S SONGS

Rhyming words, and tunes that match
  Could be a song composed
Not much like a tale that's told
  This form, considered prose.

Conveying thoughts in poetry
  With words that sound the same
Catchy phrases, that you chose
  In time will get a name.

Most times it is a long song
  That weaves a tale of woe
Why they are not happy
  And what made their feelings glow.

Old songs tell that story
  Today it's much the same
Old songs will live forever
  Because of their refrain.

9-12-08

DICTIONARY

Webster's dictionary
  Will help, if you're confused
Tells you how to spell it
  And where it can be used.

Listed alphabetically
  Are English words defined
Tells what their description is
  And how they're so inclined.

Made so you can understand
  Removing any doubt
Listed words from A to Z
  That's what it's all about.

9-9-08

ALL YEAR LONG

Christmas should be all year long
  Not only in December
Celebrated only, just one day
  To make the world remember.

His birthday is the same each year
  When stories are retold
Heaven has no calendar
  To say He's young or old.

9-10-08

REAL ESTATE

Recorded is your property
　For this you have a deed
Assessments are the tax you pay
　For services you'll need.

You could be a rancher
　With many acres, called a spread
With this you make a living
　Which helps to buy the bread.

Some folks like the city
　With people all around
Have back yards, with gardens
　And plant thing in the ground.

There are those who rather pay rent
　And don't own property
Can't afford the prices asked
　And don't want responsibility.

Buy or sell the land you own
　To fit your situation
Settle where you think is best
　There's room throughout the nation.

9-16-08

HOBBIES

It's good to have a hobby
  That fills what's called "spare time"
Pick the one that satisfies
  It could be one like mine.

Hobbies, sometimes more than one
  Could be coins or stamps
If you write much poetry
  It leads to writer's cramps.

Projects that require things
  Like wood, nails and screws
Keep you busy most the time
  Help void the Monday morning blues.

People that don't have hobbies
  Are sure to wind up bored
When you find the one you like
  A positive you scored.

9-16-08

PASTORS

How do they pick a topic??
  For a Sunday morning preach
Most likely it's inspired
  To elaborate and teach.

Each sermon is quite different
  Depending on the theme
At times it's of our Holy God
  The one who is supreme.

Details of the subject
  Are assembled to convey
What took place, so long ago
  And what takes place today.

Each pastor has a method
  Much different from the rest
Presenting scripture is their job
  With Jesus as their guest.

9-15-08

DRAFTED

When Uncle Sam has need of you
  GREETINGS it will say
Tells you that you're drafted
  In a friendly sort of way.

They don't sign off with BEST REGARDS
  To all they say the same
Basic training is in store
  Before you play their game.

In wartime this will happen
  'Til then you'll learn to kill
Teach you ways how to survive
  You'll need this kind of skill.

Enemies will do the same
  To fortify their ranks
Those not called will stay behind
  Give those who go their appreciated thanks.

9-15-08

DIPLOMA AND DEGREES

You earned what is called a diploma
  A certificate that has your name
Four years of constant study
  Much knowledge to retain.

Qualified to get a job
  Equipped with education
Must prove to those who hired you
  You're now put on probation.

If you're good, and specialize
  And earned a master degree
This could mean a raise in pay
  From your company.

Professionals will line their wall
  Diplomas by the score
When and where they added them
  In time there should be more.

Required in the world today
  A college education
Needed for the job you seek
  Is lots of information.

9-14-08

STEADFAST

When your mind is made up
  And you're steadfast in your ways
Will you make the needed changes
  When comes uncertain days???

Being steadfast, in the Lord
  You make your feelings firm
Steadfast, is your quest to know
  There's always more to learn.

Tempted by the Devil
  Be firm and don't give in
Willpower is now needed
  To keep you from his sin.

To remain and be most steadfast
  Have faith, and trust the Lord
Tell all those the GOOD NEWS truth
  HIS HOME is your reward.

9-14-08

ONE DAY AT A TIME

Unequal life you gave to all
  To live "One day at a time"
It starts on earth, the day of birth
  Just a simple life, or one of great refine.

God made the world, way back then
  Completely free of sin
And like today, the war goes on
  When the Devil enters in.

So what He did, was sent His Son
  To show us how to live
Most lessons that He taught us
  Was how to love, and to forgive.

One day He'll call believers home
  With no more pain or strife
Happiness is yours alone
  When you lead a GODLY life.

5-11-08

POWER OF PRAYER

When doctors say there is no hope
  And deem your chances rare
Tried everything that's possible
  Steps in the power of prayer.

Lots of remedies and experiments
  New methods they will try
What worked well for others
  Are medicines you'll buy.

Keep looking for a miracle
  For something they can't cure
Answered prayers, from God alone
  Can once more make you pure.

Prayer has worked so many times
  It's hard to list them all
Those endowed will say it's true
  With stories, they recall.

9-15-08

My wife Martha (right) with her parents, Julia and William Bachman and little sister Julia. (circa 1935)

HO   HO   HO

I'm Elmer the Elf
  I make all the toys
To fill up the shelf
  For the good little boys,

Mrs. Santa Claus
  Will take care of the girls
She has many presents
  As a list she unfurls.

Santa's red underwear
  Is now nice and clean
Mrs. Claus took it from
  The washing machine

His red suit is off
  To the tailor it went
He'll wear it next year
  If others don't rent.

He says HO HO HO
  To his reindeer he talks
When they won't pull his sleigh
  Then surly, he walks.

He'll come down your chimney
  And fill up your socks
And if you're not good
  You might get just ROCKS.

It's back home, to rest
  After one busy night
He'll say MERRY CHRISTMAS
  And wish you all good night.

HURRYCAINS
OR
HURRICANES

Hurricanes will inundate
  With heavy rains in store
Destruction in the path they take
  Is seen when they hit shore.

Many storms that form at sea
  Will take the same direction
Boarded windows and store fronts
  Are shut, to give protection.

This takes place when seas get warm
  They last until November
Many of the blows that hit
  I'm sure that you'll remember.

Repairs are made by those involved
  Piles of rubbish, they will burn
Prayers are offered up, with hope
  The storms will not return.

9-25-08

OBLIGATION

Pay back time is now in store
  For all things I was given
Picnics, shopping and doctor visits
  The many places I was driven.

When the shoe is on the other foot
  You'll even up the score
Perhaps in time, you will have needs
  So left open, is the door.

I'm sure that we are obligated
  To God, for love and grace
Jesus Christ paid all our debts
  For sins, He took our place.

We'll always keep the felling of
  Our thanks, and obligation
He is the one who keeps us fit
  With constant rehabilitation.

9-25-08

BELIEVE IT OR NOT

Looking for the unusual
  Surprised at what you find
Oddities, in all shapes and forms
  Are just one of a kind.

These happenings rare, when you compare
  Each different from the rest
God loves all His creations
  What we call worst, or best.

Ripley looks for what's not norm
  Displays fill his museums
Many of the "BELIEVE IT OR NOTS"
  Are still called human beings.

Our graceful God, someday will change
  Disabled will be healed
Promises to His faithful flock
  In time will be revealed.

4-5-09

CRITICS

Critics now are ten times ten
　Perhaps there's many more
All kinds of entertainment
　It's hard for most to score.

Actors try to make it real
　In roles that they portray
Situations are the theme
　That could happen any day.

Trouble, sure, will lead the rest
　Put there to make you sad
When the hurt is over and fixed
　The ending finds all glad.

In real life there are times of hurt
　Filled with lots of grief
That's the time to realize
　The test of your belief.

4-5-09

SELF CONSCIOUS

When people try to justify
  What other people see
Self consciousness has taken hold
  From limelight, they will flee.

Clothes must match from head to toe
  Or else they make a change
Wardrobe full, to choose what's right
  Won't wear things that look strange.

Men get upset when hair falls out
  Most costly to replace
They let it grow on chin and cheeks
  Still grows good, on the face.

9-1-08

GUARDIAN

Guardians give protection
  To keep us from great harm
Some are angels in disguise
  That answer our alarm.

"Guardian Angels" is a group
  That help to keep the peace
In a place where crime exists
  They soon might make it cease.

Those involved get little pay
  For a great job that they do
Unarmed heroes that apply
  Are picked from quite a few.

If you become a Guardian
  And rear a child not yours
Protection in their time of need
  Is what this word implores.

8-30-08

DETERMINE

When stumbling blocks get in your way
  And goals get hard to reach
Determination must take place
  That's what statistics teach.

Discouragement will make you think
  you have but little chance
Determination is the fuel
  To make your drive advance.

Concentrate, perhaps regroup
  And find the right direction
You satisfied all things you tried
  Results don't need perfection.

8-30-08

STEALING

Stealing shows great profit
  Can be costly when you're caught
You broke God's 8TH commandment
  And you did it all for naught.

It could start with little things
  Then soon could multiply
Why you didn't pay for it
  Most likely you will lie.

Punishment for such a feat
  Some times might be severe
They cut off little fingers
  Perhaps a piece of ear.

When you take what is not yours
  You're placed in jeopardy
When cost is high on what you stole
  It becomes a felony.

8-30-08

FEEBLE

Feeble is the term most used
  For the weak when they grow old
When in time you reach that stage
  Must stay out of the cold.

Memories of yesterdays
  Are lost and seem to fade
Can't comprehend and can't make plans
  When young they could have made.

Most need care, they can not share
  The things most others do
Growing old will slow things down
In time, it's me and you

8-30-08

ESTIMATE

When there is an estimate
  It comes close to the cost to fix
Labor and materials
  Plus the paint you mix.

Even though it's not your fault
  At times you have to pay
Part of what it costs to fix
  To get things underway.

All policies will differ
  Depending what you spend
Companies that insure you
  Make estimates their trend,

8-30-08

FRUSTRATION

Frustration comes to those who fail
  To accomplish what they start
Some folks jump that hurdle
  Because they're very smart.

Free from worry and concern
  Of what led to this condition
Lots of prayers and quiet time
  Restored is your ambition.

8-30-08

240

BURDENS

When a monkey is on your back
  A burden could be yours
Advantage now the Devil takes
  He hopes this time he scores.

Prayer should help you overcome
  The thing that got you down
Remember if you win the race
  The prize might be a crown.

Bad situations surly will take place
  Be ready for a fight
Pray to God that sin won't win
  Then burdens will take flight.

8-29-08

CALCULATORS AND PROBLEMS

Problems come to all at times
  Some times high are the steaks
The bottom line should make things fine
  If no one makes mistakes.

Calculators do the work
  And help to solve things fast
When you don't apply your skill
  Results could be the past.

Must put on your thinking cap
  When it's calculating time
Problem don't care who they pick
  They could be yours or mine.

8-29-08

BASHFUL

Bashful people are most shy
  They blush and face turns red
Because they're on the tender side
  React to what you said.

Being bashful is no sin
  It's made up in your genes
At times it might delay a trend
  And hold up ways and means.

It will get lost in time
  Some attitudes will fade
Until then it's yours alone
  Cause that's the way you're made.

8-29-08

AMBITION

Ambition hits an all time high
  When you're feeling good
The times when you're not up to par
  Stagnation understood.

Give your all and then some more
  Do ever what it takes
Push yourself until you're tired
  And hope that nothing breaks.

Ambitious people get ahead
  They go the extra mile
When you achieve the goal you set
  I'll bet that you will smile

8-29-08

DOMAIN

If your home is now your castle
  And your king of your domain
You may have the final word
  While others will complain.

Rules you make are good for all
  Your just in what you do
Keep them guessing what comes next
  Cause they don't have a clue.

Someone has to make the rules
  To keep an upright crew
Punishment will be handed out!
  It might as well be you.

8-29-08

ENCOURGE

Encourage those who lag behind
  To do the best they can
Remember all the times you fell
  Now you can say "I RAN."

Start out slow then build the pace
  In time they will improve
They will lose self consciousness
  Your goal was to remove.

Encouragement is positive
  To help all find their way
Satisfaction you will have
  Each and every day.

8-29-08

DWINDLE

A little here, a little there
  The pile will soon get small
When you dwindle what you have
  You're headed for a fall.

Money seems to top the list
  If spent it won't be long
Bills mount up and soon you'll sing
  The poor mans favorite song.

"OH WE AINT GOT A BARREL OF MONEY"
  At times we wish we had
Just because you dwindled
  Now things are looking bad.

8-29-08

ENDURE

Ailments pain and suffering
  At times we must endure
Hope and pray that scientists
  Will some day find a cure.

Mother Nature has a hand
  To make things cure themselves
Just in case it don't work out
  Keep medicine on the shelf.

We all need treatment now and then
  To keep us feeling fine
Doctors say you will feel good
  If you some time drink red wine.

8-29-08

CIRCUMSTANCES

Circumstance is what you say
　Could that be your excuse?
Overcome what did go wrong
　You've gained freedom from abuse.

When you're small and don't control
　What others do to you
Some have many situations
　You most likely had a few.

Avoid forbidden circumstance
　No trouble will you see
Enjoy surroundings that you have
　Then happy you will be.

8-29-08

CULTIVATE

Take time to care and cultivate
  With tender love and care
Think of all the things God has made
  And those you'd like to share.

To make things grow you must cultivate
  Or else it just might die
Since you know what must be done
  And know the reason why.

Pruning, primping what you have
  Are steps along the way
A product that you will enjoy
  When it comes harvest day.

8-29-08

TRAGEDY

A tragedy some times could be
  A blessing in disguise
God makes the change that He thinks best
  In time you'll realize.

Upset you are when things don't jell
  Most likely there's a reason
When the time is right you'll know
  He's never out of season.

Saddened and you don't know why
  It's not someone else but me
It could be a test of faith
  You'll have to wait and see.

If He calls a loved one home
  You sit and wonder why
Filled with grief that lasts awhile
  The sadness makes you cry.

Gladdened are your future thoughts
  While leaning on His promise
Proving that His word is truth
  Was a guy called "DOUBTING THOMAS."

8-27-08

My wedding to Martha, June 10, 1951.

PRETENDING

Pretending to be happy
  Takes on an actor's role
Reflect great charm and laugh a lot
  Make known you're in control.

Impress your friends with odds and ends
  Displayed so all can see
You know the way to set the stage
  Now coy as one might be.

Let folks know you've lots of dough
  You have so many things
Unpaid bills, your mailbox fills
  Each day the mailman brings.

The hole gets deep, it's hard to sleep
  Pent up with foolish pride
Must rearrange and make a change
  The truth no longer hides.

There is a way, to God I pray
  His guidance I employ
With His love and Son above
  At last I'll find real joy.

8-10-98

DOUBTS

Thomas had to be convinced
  Because he had a doubt
Proof he needed positive
  No facts could be left out.

Things that happen every day
  Some phony, to deceive
Filled with empty promises
  To convince you to believe.

When you need to be convinced
  Proof will make it so
Until then when you have doubts
  All facts you want to know.

8-23-08

HARMONY

Harmony, a simple word
  A blend of many things
It could be the barber shop quartet
  Four part harmony it sings.

Those who work in harmony
  Reach out and hope to find
An answer to a problem
  And solve what's on their mind.

It's said two heads are better
  When something must be done
Will satisfy a group that's large
  Instead of pleasing one.

8-25-08

PROCRASTINATION

Procrastinate and put things off
  Can be one's own life style
Jobs that should be done today
  Are put off for a while.

Perhaps I'll get it done real soon
  YEAH! That's when I'll get it done
Don't have time to mess with it
  While I am having fun.

That's what I said some time ago
  When doing came to mind
Why I didn't do it???
  The time still hard to find.

Do it now, don't let things ride
  It helps you keep the pace
Procrastinate and let things go
  You'll never win a race.

8-24-08

AMERICAN

Once they lived in foreign lands
   In so many different places
Now they are American
   A mixture of all races.

Some are black and most are white
   Asian groups now live here too
They like the freedom that we have
   And wave red, white, and blue.

Most go to school and specialize
   And work what they like best
They like the democratic ways we have
   Then learn how to invest.

Most succeed and fill a need
   Since once they were held back
Their offspring born American
   Will keep all things intact.

8-24-08

BORROWING

I need this and I need that
   I'll give it back tomorrow
Special tools to do a job
   Are some things we might borrow.

We borrow in emergency
   To make it work again
Friends don't mind to lend things out
   If only now and then.

When you need it more than once
   Why still insist to borrow?
Go find that item that you'll need
   And purchase it tomorrow.

8-23-08

SECOND HAND

Buy used things that still work good
   Could save you quite a penny
We can't afford to buy all what's new
   Because there are so many.

Shop around, look every where
   If lucky you will find
What you need and can afford
   The thing you had in mind.

People will update the things they have
   Sell off what's second hand
TV's and cars are on the list
   They're sold throughout the land.

When you find just what you need
   And at a price that's right
It could last for quite a while
   And fit a budget tight.

8-23-08

PROMISES

Broken are the promises
  And the vows we make
When you are not satisfied
  In time you will forsake.

When two people don't agree
  And take a different course
That's the time they separate
  And wind up in divorce.

If our God would act like this
  Where could we put our trust
Hope would fade and sad we are
  Our bubble now would bust.

Our hope is in His promise
  The Bible tells us so
It's a fact of that we're sure
  You'll find out when you go.

8-22-08

UTOPIA

Utopia can not be found
  No matter where you go
All is never perfect
  When surroundings never glow.

One place is hot, the other cold
  It changes all the time
In between it's moderate
  And folks just find this fine.

Scattered are the people
  Who live in different places
Speak a language of their own
  And make up all the races.

Some are yellow, others red
  We know there's black and white
Most work throughout the day time
  And sleep in dark of night.

Searching for that special place
  Will stop when all seems well
Make new friends and settle in
  And that is where you'll dwell.

8-22-08

ANGELS

Many angels do God's will
  You find them near and far
Some of them are black not white
  They even drive a car.

Once a favorite angel
  Wanted God's equal power
God said "no" and threw him out
  Now souls he will devour.

Sent to hell that's where he'll dwell
  Until our Christ returns
No more will he bother us
  We rejoice when Satan burns.

At times we will be tempted
  This surely leads to sin
Trust the Lord and follow Him
  He'll teach you how to win.

8-19-08

CONSIDERATE

Being not considerate
  Is a selfish act
Do what ever satisfies
  And seldom give things back.

I want this, and I want that
  Is all you'll ever hear
Unkind folks who act like this
  I'd rather not be near.

Friends they don't have many
  It's not hard to reason why
Friends will not associate
  Even after one more try.

8-20-08

REHAB

Rehab puts you back in shape
  It makes what's weak get strong
Fix the action that you lost
  It helps to aid what's wrong.

When you had a lethal blow
  You need some time to rest
Now it's time to rise again
  And put strength to test.

Simple movements first are slow
  Persistence does the trick
Perhaps in time you will feel fine
  \And use no walking stick

8-18-08

POM POM GIRLS

Cheering makes a team fight hard
  \Even when they lose
Heal the pain and pass out towels
  To ease the losing blues.

Pom-pom girls in scanty clothes
  Are dressed to get attention
Sexy moves that all can see
  And more than I can mention.

Shapely girls from far and wide
  Apply to be selected
Those not picked might shed a tear
  And feel they were neglected.

Football teams have girls that cheer
  They move fast when it's cold
Must move on when beauty fades
  And leave when they get old.

8-19-08

IF

If means that it might have been
  Possibilities by the score
How, what, where, or when
  Make the changes, if not sure.

The door is left wide open
  When deciding what to do
If you have the final word
  The finger points at you.

Monday morning quarterbacks
  Are "Iffy" all the time
There would be no losers
  And most things would be fine.

Saying IF when things go wrong
  You'd like a second chance
The choice you make would be okay
  IF you knew things in advance.

IF I don't end thoughts on IF
  And IF I did not care
Remembering IF I don't forget
  The "IF WORD" that I share.

8-17-08

LITTER

Along the road are plastic bags
  Filled with trash called litter
Thrown by those who could care less
  This act makes me quite bitter.

An old beer can that once was full
  Such things that had their use
"Keep our country beautiful"
  Abstain from this abuse.

If you're caught you'll pay the fine
  It's meant to teach a lesson
Smaller plastic bags you'll see
  When slobs quit all that messing.

8-18-08

LANGUAGE

Bad language used in yester years
  Was said and not dad-nab-it
Circumstance or sudden pain
  Pops up that old bad habit.

Some can't talk without bad words
  To stress what's on their mind
Gutter talk is all they know
  They know no other kind.

Education sure can help
  Along with fear of God
Trust, faith, and power of prayer
  Can be your lightning rod.

Most outgrow bad language
  For some it will remain
We can live without it
  Cause it adulterates our grain.

8-14-08

LOST OR MISSING

When a loved one you can't find
  Abducted, if not lost
Prayer and hope for safe return
  Regardless of the cost.

It could happen anywhere
  At times you least expect
Although you are most careful
  And try not to neglect.

What is said I'll say again
  It's meant so you remind
Youth are fooled by evil ones
  With words that seem most kind.

Just an ounce of prevention
  Is worth a pound of cure
Tell your young not to accept
  What seems a harmless lure.

8-15-08

PICTURES TAKEN

Pictures taken long ago
  Remind us of those days
What we did and how we felt
  And how we changed our ways.

Photographs of black and white
  Before color took its place
Photos now are digital
  With those who keep the pace.

Simple cameras like a box
  With time was modified
Added was the distance lens
  The one that you could slide.

Albums filled with photos
  Show how we grew in time
Videos now added
  Are used by yours and mine.

8-16-08

SONGS OF OLD

Songs of old had simple words
  With many about the moon
Rhyming words that all could sing
  Like moon, spoon, croon, and tune.

Rock and roll is here to stay
  It don't have much romance
Ballads from a Broadway show
  Your love life may enhance.

Country music now the thing
  Fits in with gospel songs
Desperate writers are confused
  Don't know where it belongs.

I hope songs of the future
  Will go back to that old craze
We need inspired writers
  To bring back those good old days.

8-16-08

THE CROSS

The cross remains a symbol
  To remind how Jesus died
Although He was most innocent
  Condemned the crucified.

He was made to carry a heavy cross
  On the road to Calvary
Nails driven through His hands and feet
  Then hung upon a tree.

Mocked Him, called him king of Jews
  And spit into his face
He suffered much upon the cross
  His blood our sins erased.

A crown of thorns placed on His head
  When called the king of Jews
Most thought it was appropriate
  To make all who watched amused.

Much wisdom taught by Jesus
  When He became a man
He told them of the Father
  And said the great "I AM."

God's plan began at Christmas
  When Virgin Mary birth'd God's Son
From death he rose a Easter time
  And proved a victory won.

Right now he's back in heaven
  With scars that still remain
Our troubled world waits patiently
  Till He returns again.

UNEQUAL LIFE

Unequal life you gave to all
  To live one day at a time
It starts on earth the day of birth
  Just a simple life, or one of great refine.

God made His world way back then
  Completely free of sin
And like today the war goes on
  When the Devil enters in.

So what He did was sent His Son
  To show us how to live
Most lessons that He taught us
  Was to love and to forgive.

One day he'll call believers home
  With no more pain or strife
Happiness is yours alone
  When you live a Godly life.

8-2-08

WATER

Taken much for granted
  Is the water that we use
Lakes are filled with lots of it
  From clear to vivid blues.

H2O is what it's called
  Its found in many things
Drinking water is the best
  That flows from natural springs.

Wash your body, cook your food
  It makes your clothes come clean
When heated past the boiling point
  The energy is steam.

We can't live without it
  No matter how we try
When all loved things don't have enough
  They shrivel up and die.

8-16-08

275

SQUARE MEALS

Three square meals at a table round
  Morning, noon, and night
Discuss events and news of the day
  Enjoy and never fight.

Nourishment is what we need
  And that is why we eat
Keeps the hungry satisfied
  With fitness to compete.

For living things it's much the same
  Neglect will make them die
Once you passed that certain stage
  Recovery you can't buy.

So fight all ills and take your pills
  They'll keep you going strong
Pharmacies keep us supplied
  The list is very long.

8-12-08

CONCERNED

Concerned means that you worry
  When the outcome is not clear
Prayer will help to ease your mind
  Remember God is near.

Petition GOD to make things well
  With prayer He will decide
His love and grace we welcome
  In Him we must abide.

It will happen any way
  According to His plan
With out His help we can not do
  He always says "I CAN."

8-13-08

KEEPING SLIM

If you increase your appetite
  And eat what comes your way
You'll be surprised the pounds you gained
  When comes the time to weigh.

Once you get past fifty
  There's one thing you should know
If you over feed your face
  Your middle sure will grow.

Much junk food and soda pop
  Will make your pounds increase
If you want to lose some weight
  These items you must cease.

It takes will power and nutrition
  Maybe health foods you will buy
Many are the diet plans
  You might give them a try.

Eat good food and exercise
  Is what they recommend
Listen what statistics say
  Over eating is a trend.

7-26-08

HOME

The many places that you lived
  Are places you called home
Most times it's shared with others
  Or by yourself alone.

It is a place you hang your hat
  You own and have a deed
Inside there is security
  With all comforts of your need.

Where you work and do what's good
  You were hired for you skills
Not only did you like it
  It more than paid the bills.

If per chance your company moves
  Into another state
That is the time to pack your bags
  Your home must relocate.

Once again it will take time
  New friendships you will win
Again it will be your happy home
  Once you're settled in.

7-26-08

FINAL BOW

When the roll is called up yonder
  And you're still not on the list
You might be there tomorrow
  That is when you will be missed.

While you're waiting for that time
  Enjoy what you have now
The days will soon be quick enough
  To make your final bow.

There is a reason why we live
  Then some day why we die
Our home on earth don't last that long
  Until that mansion in the sky.

8-5-08

HANG LOOSE

Tomorrow is the future
  It goes on for years and years
We don't know what each day will hold
  Some times it's filled with tears.

Sixty plus the average
  For some it could be less
Fate controlled by God above
  He'll put you through the test.

Like weather there's no guarantee
  Each moment we're uncertain
Many changes will take place
  Until that final curtain.

Adventure with each passing day
  Is what we have in store
Complaining makes you ill at heart
  The challenge is no more.

Be of good cheer and just "Hang Loose"
  An old Hawaiian phrase
Remember what God promised you
  Then much brighter are your days.

8-6-08

WALKING

First we creep then we crawl
  Soon after that we walk
Try to copy all what grownups do
  Communicate with talk.

The need to go from place to place
  Walking still the thing
When you get quite good at it
  No longer do you cling.

Upright standing on two feet
  God made man like himself
Gave him brains so he could attain
  Improvements on his health.

Walking is required
  In all things that we do
Doctors say it's good for you
  Even when you're ninety two.

Keep on walking, strut your stuff
  You need it every day
Join those who do it constantly
  When old age comes their way.

7-26-08

HOPELESS

Hopeless means there is no chance
  You've reached the bitter end
All is gone, there is no more
  There's nothing to defend.

It took time to reach that point
  You moaned and groaned for years
Happiness you could not find
  Was hid when you shed tears.

You had your fling. did everything
  Suggested by your peers
At party time you over did
  And had too many beers.

There is still time to change your life
  Regardless of your style
Take time to read the Bible
  And find out life is worthwhile.

7-26-08

BELLS

Flashing lights and bells that ring
  Are made to get attention
Used for all emergencies
  The list too long to mention.

Ambulances will flash lights and ring a bell
  And speed to get there quick
Time is most essential
  To aid you when you're sick.

Fire trucks do much the same
  Each time with each alarm
Rescue those who might be trapped
  Keep others from all harm.

We ring bells at New Year's time
  For both the old and new
At times they're rung at weddings
  When hitching time is through.

Bells toll when life is no more
  They're never out of season
When they're rung you can be sure
  They're rung for one good reason.

7-28-08

TRAVELING

So many different places
  That lie beyond the sea
Each one reflects its beauty
  When visiting you'll see.

Different customs, different styles
  It changes where you go
Down to the hot equator
  Or far up north with snow.

In your travels you may find
  A place you'd like to live
Not too hot and not too cold
  Much thought you'll have to give.

When traveling, you will see a lot
  Could be in Greece or Rome
When you return once more you'll say
  It's good to be back home.

7-28-08

PRACTICE

Practice each and every day
  Although you do quite well
Constant practice is the key
  In time you will excel.

If you like what you do well
  Enjoyment you will find
Others that participate
  Are soon left far behind.

Talent scouts are on the prowl
  All sports look for new faces
If you're picked because you're good
  You'll travel to new places.

When in time a pro you'll be
  Your earnings will be great
Practice made this possible
  No longer must you wait.

7-22-08

DECEPTION

Deception comes in many forms
  The Devil knows them all
You could be outwitted
  Soon be headed for a fall.

Deception is his middle name
  The Devil does it well
He'll teach you how to flirt with sin
  And join him down in hell.

Long ago God favored him
  And treated him quite well
He tried to have the power of God
  Was punished and sent to hell.

He will continue to be active
  Until our Lord returns
That's when all the dead will rise
  And cheer when Satan burns.

7-23-08

QUESTIONS

The young ask many questions
  While learning as they grow
Of how it works and what it does
  All things they want to know.

Most times you know the answer
  And you still ask quite a few
Both look for a good reason
  And ask why skies are blue.

Learning is a process
  On that you can depend
Accumulated knowledge
  The search that has no end.

Questions asked throughout your life
  You ask and wonder why
Keep looking for that answer
  Until the day you die.

7-23-08

LATE

Being late a habit
  Once started hard to break
Most times you are quite tardy
  For appointments that you make.

"Better late than never"
  Will satisfy a few
Don't set well with others
  In all things that you do.

Even when you have to wait
  It pays to be on time
If you're late the word gets out
  You're guilty of that crime.

7-23-08

NO HAIR

We're born most times without it
  With age, men's heads get bare
In time the color changes
  Don't care, 'cause it's still there.

When young some men might lose it
  The trend is shave it clean
Those who want to save it
  Look for that magic cream.

Companies take your money
  Say we'll restore your hair
If you do believe them
  You'll pay a price that's fair.

Science says it's in your genes
  That's why you're not endowed
Could be that you're masculine
  Be bald and still be proud.

Some men are most self-conscious
  When their head gets bare
On one side they grow it long
  To cover what's not there.

Being bald is not too bad
  If healthy you may be
When you repeat the process
  You are part of history.

7-24-08

OXYGEN

Air we breathe has oxygen
  It makes our blood run clean
Damaged lungs need more of it
  It's fed through a machine.

Mix 2 parts with hydrogen
  The gases are now wet
Nature has the formula
  Now water is what you get.

Pure oxygen makes the fire real hot
  It also makes steel rust
The slow process under oceans
  Soon will form an ugly crust.

Vegetation, trees, and such
  Keep us well supplied
Where there's air you'll find it
  It has no place to hide.

8-16-08

THINKING YOUNG

The body old with memories young
　Remembering what unfurls
Still take the time to look and dream
　While watching shapely girls.

Can't forget the good old days
　Still have that roving eye
Looking for that certain one
　Of this I can't deny.

Although the fire is burning low
　It burns both day and night
With age you have to take the count
　Or else you'll lose the fight.

There were so many things you did
　You gave them all a try
So keep adventures going strong
　Until the day you die.

8-17-08

SCRIPTURE

Scripture in the Bible
  Perhaps one time on scroll
Inspired by the hand of God
  And facts and records told.

It starts with God's creation
  Ends with glory when we die
Relating thoughts and wisdom
  That we could never buy.

The first part is before our Lord
  With tales of what took place
How God created Heaven and Earth
  And blessings He called grace.

Each word was carefully written
  To make each phrase quite clear
Interpreters give different views
  Each message that you hear.

Writers alter what is said
  They try so hard to please
Made scripture reading easier
  By ridding thous and these.

9-18-08

CONTAMINATE

The Devil will contaminate
  What ever comes his way
Drop your guard and take a chance
  His game you soon will play.

Little effort to avoid
  Will open up his door
His antics seem like harmless fun
  They make you look for more.

Friends you know who act like this
  Want you to do the same
Give into pressure they apply
  You'll shovel coal in his hall of flame.

God knows the Devil inside out
  Dealt with him for many years
He'll show you how to rid his hold
  And welcome joyful tears.

9-17-08

WATCHFUL

Taking care of things held dear
  Is filled with TLC
Watchful eyes that fill the needs
  Much help to them will be.

Possessions will last longer
  When proper care is done
Energy that is spent this way
  Should be lots of fun.

The owner is responsible
  Most watchful they must be
Time well spent is worth the cost
  It could be a pet or a tree.

12-11-08

HERBICIDE

The Bible is an herbicide
  To kill the weeds in life
Cutting into the mindful soul
  With words sharp as a knife.

Wisdom, lessons, good advice
  It covers everything
The outcome of sinful ways
  In offerings, what to bring.

Stories told are gospel truth
  Who lived on earth that time
Stones were used as punishment
  Disobeyers were turned to brine.

Read it once or maybe more
  It has the Godly trend
The words will have more meaning
  As we try to comprehend.

12-12-08

MEEK

Meek and humble, weak or strong
   Knowing the Lord is a winner's song.

When you stray you'll pay the price
   Depending how you live
Forgiveness, plus another chance
   The Lord will always give.

Regardless, all that you might be
   In time, you're sure to die
Until the day God calls you home
   You best eat humble pie.

Seek eternal life in heaven
   It should be your only goal
Praise the Lord for showing us
   That forever lives your soul.

7-4-09

GUARDIAN

I must have a guardian
  Who watches over me
Could be a God sent angel
  Or one I can not see.

Countless times my guardian
  Saved me, made me safe
Ever since, until this day
  When I was just a waif.

Prayers of thanks are given
  To God, who is in charge
He sends all the guardians
  Their job is small or large.

Countless times they helped me
  I'm here and still alive
We all need God's guardians
  That is how we all survive.

7-2-09

KINGDOM

If there was no kingdom
  There would be no king to rule
Pay taxes due, and rules for all
  And hopefully, not cruel.

Just before His crucifixion
  Jesus was called "THE KING OF JEWS"
Now He's back in heaven
  Still spreading all "GOOD NEWS."

His kingdom is forever
  No queen will ever share
When life on earth is over
  His kingdom you will share.

4-5-09

GUIDANCE

A constant search for guidance
  So we don't go astray
You'll find the answer in the Lord
  The truth, the light and way.

Leaning on His every word
  His wisdom and His power
The need is always yours to have
  Every minute, day, or hour.

Through the ages, up 'til now
  He's always very near
Thank Him, praise Him always
  A prayer, He likes to hear.

4-5-09

INTERCEDE

When the world was on a downfall
  God knew there was a need
His Son was sent to Earth from heaven
  With plans to intercede.

A sacrifice that some still doubt
  It was the only way
Made His Son alive again
  Jesus Christ is here to stay.

What to do, and how to live
  Many stories that He told
Soon He had believers
  That were both young and old.

6-28-09

SPIRIT

Spirit could mean many things
   The list is very long
When HOLY used in front of it
   To God it must belong.

Spirit says just how you fell
   Unhappy or you're glad
Expression might fool every one
   When smiling, you're still mad.

When you need a lift in life
   To make your spirit high
Say a prayer to God above
   The one you ought to try.

If you're poor in spirit
   At happiness you're guessing
That's the time to praise the Lord
   He's sure to add a blessing.

7-3-09

REVELATION

When the world was looking for
  A way to revelation
God sent down His only Son
  With hopes He'd reach all nations.

Missionaries do this job
  And teach as He would do
When the call is strong enough
  It could be me or you.

Obstacles, like language
  Many dangers may come your way
Spread the word of God's "GOOD NEWS"
  No matter where you stay.

Hungry to know more of God
  And promises of Jesus
The revelation of your soul
  Will make our effort please us.

7-11-09

Martha and me at our son Bill's wedding, 2005

LISTEN

God's voice may be a whisper
  And yet, the deaf can hear it clear
He may seem so far away
  But he is very near.

Wanting all the ones He loves
  To listen to his voice
His Son will tell you how to live
  I pray that is your choice.

Jesus was God's sacrifice
  To stop the Devil's works
Temptation is his motive
  Round the corner, where it lurks.

How to keep us free from sin
  Like any father, he must scold
When sometime in the future
  Your hand he'd like to hold.

7-12-09

WISE

When you are wise, and your choice is right
   You'll sing a happy song
If you're wrong, you pay the price
   With a tearful face that's long.

Wrongs and errors, plus many trials
   A lesson learned each time
Experience come from all you did
   Your try to make things rhyme.

Rules to follow can be had
   From one who tried all things
The wise old owl now has answers
   Is what this message brings.

7-13-09

UNIVERSE

Considered a speck in the universe
  Our God picked this special place
Included were the elements
  To sustain the human race.

His perfect world was given choice
  Soon temptation led to sin
The Devil made his presence known
  He had his first known win.

Modern man, not satisfied
  Made exploits to the moon
Back on earth where he fits in
  More outreach will be soon.

With population on the rapid rise
  How long will this world last ????
He will seek more places in outer space
  Each time there is a blast.

7-15-09

PRAISE

Praise to God, the angels sing
  Their voices raised on high
The multitude that flap their wings
  Fill up the heavenly sky.

Choirs of angels, they are called
  With great faith they earned their wings
Harmony that fills the air
  Each time their message sings.

Singing some hymns, old or new
  Each note could ring a bell
Keeps the Devil in his place
  In his dungeon, down in hell.

If we try to imitate
  The singing of their song
Same quality, we cannot get
  In time we might belong.

7-16-09

SOURCE

All things have a source
  Some place where they must start
God gave Moses rules of ten
  Now we must do our part.

Jesus was the source from God
  When darkness filled the world
He was the light, to make things right
  His righteousness unfurled.

Primary things will form the source
  The start that has the need
That's why God sent Jesus
  To help us grow from seed.

Growing in His truthful Word
  There's always room for more
The Bible has the answers
  That will raise up high, YOUR SCORE!

7-17-09

PATTERN

A pattern is quite necessary
  To duplicate or fit
Frustrated would be those who sew
  Not forgetting those who knit.

Man sure has a pattern
  Duplicates his work and eats
Most the time, he will repeat
  Each day that he completes.

Many projects are in need
  So they come out just the same
With out patterns we'd be lost
  And considered to be lame.

Many patterns formed by God
  When he created man
Made many colors to fit in
  Count as many as you can.

Different languages and places
  Some hot or very cold
Missionaries spread God's word
  The sweetest story every told.

7-18-09

SPIRITUALLY

When spiritually you pray to God
  In a way that it should be
Your soul lifts up with blessings
  Then much happiness you'll see.

Being spiritual don't take much
  A habit you must form
The Devil tries to intercede
  With pleasures, or a storm.

Constant prayer will stop him cold
  This weapon we must use
At times his charm will tempt us
  The Bible is our fuse.

It's good to let all others know
  Being spiritual is the answer
The one from hell will now retreat
  Be no longer a tempting dancer.

7-19-09

VOICE

The first time that you use your voice
  Is when you're born and cry
Imitate the sounds you hear
  Start talking, bye and bye.

Accent of the ones you hear
  Will always stay with you
Many sounds that seem so strange
  There are more than a few

It is the way we communicate
  Most living things may have a voice
Make sounds, but cannot talk
  It was His utmost choice.

Spoken is the word of God
  His Holy Spirit sometimes roars
Your Bible can give the answer
  To each question it explores.

7-18-09

PARADISE

Advertisement calls it paradise
  When you live there, life's the same
Hawaiians do the hula
  Dance with torches lit with flame.

Not like the heaven God promised us
  It has weather, warm and clear
Gives comfort to all visitors
  Cause it's the same throughout the year.

The sneaky attack of the Japanese
  Caused havoc and destroyed
The loss of life and Navy ships
  Made Americans annoyed.

Still Hawaiians' love is so genuine
  I found this to be so
Tourists that have visited
  Will say so, when they go.

Like the real paradise, it does come very close
  Still lacks so many things
It can't compare to God's paradise
  Is what this message brings.

7-18-09

JUSTIFIED

When reasoning seems most justified
  Then compassion should step in
Inspired by the love of God
  Is where it should begin.

Even when we do respond
  To what might hurt our pride
All God's creatures need respect
  Learn to take this in your stride.

Only God is justified
  His love He gives to all
To creatures He created
  On this celestial ball.

7-19-09

INFLUENCE

Christ Jesus is my influence
  He makes my feelings soar
Lifts my spirits when I'm down
  His love I can't ignore.

Peers could be your influence
  That lead you far astray
Picking those who know the Lord
  Should be your only way.

The Devil tries his influence
  With many harmless tricks
That's the time to seek the Lord
  Your problems he will fix.

You could be an influence
  By sharing God's "GOOD NEWS"
When you find someone that's down
  His word will chase the blues.

7-19-09

REGENERATION

Back sliders must return to school
　They need God's education
Again restore a firm belief
　It's called regeneration.

When you drift, lose sight of God
　The Devil will take over
The Bible helps you anchor fast
　You'll stay in fields of clover.

Regeneration and revival
　Is what this message brings
A second chance God gives to all
　Is what the angel sings.

7-19-09

ETERNITY

Eternity is forever
  No beginning or no end
The choice is yours, alone to spend
  With God's foe, or Son and friend.

Waiting for that glorious day
  In time, it can be yours
While living make the most of it
  Included with God's chores.

Not all people have this fate
  It all depends on you
God will help you reach that goal
  When your life on earth is through.

We count the days, that turn into years
  Some have many, some have few
Time stands still in heaven
  Where the sky is always blue.

7-21-09

SUBSTANTIAL

When substantial is the evidence
  The defense might raise a doubt
Unless there is a witness
  In what their job is all about.

Common sense should play the part
  Of what has taken place
Majority of those involved
  Decides who won the case.

Guilty ones sometimes go free
  By distortion of the facts
Proof will be disqualified
  Because of all it lacks.

Substantial is the word of God
  Inspired throughout the Bible
No one can raise a single doubt
  That makes our great God liable.

7-21-09

AWESOME

Beyond the term of being great
  The title now is awesome
You can call our Great God this
  For all the things that He has done.

When you can't get any greater
  And can't find another name
Awesome is the answer
  It has power, and has fame.

Looks like awesome is here to stay
  A most creative word
It fits the workings of our God
  Forever it will be heard.

7-21-09

RIVAL

The Devil is God's rival
  That no one can debate
God kicked him out of heaven
  When he tried to imitate.

Since then he's been a foe of God
  And wants to take the lead
He lures Christ Jesus followers
  With clever tricks, indeed.

Temptation his big weapon
  The bait that catches many
Finds God's people hard to locate
  Just like a two tail penny.

The Devil is sure to act like this
  Until our Lord returns.
That's the time he'll be no more
  Down in hell, with rubbish burns.

7-21-09

INQUISITIVE

"What you don't know can't hurt you."
  This phrase you should ignore
When you are inquisitive
  You'll open every door.

Lurking in the shadows
  Might be trouble and despair
Even when it tries to hide
  The culprit is still there.

Inquisitiveness is a quest of man
  That started long ago
How it works, and what it does
  His motive is to know.

Why we live, then some day die
  Replaced by someone new
Why this cycle has no end
  That started with a few.

Why God favored earth for man
  Took care of all his needs
Why he harvests chosen ones
  And throws away all weeds.

7-21-08

MEDICINE

Many are the miracles
  That medicine can do
Shots to build immunity
  Perhaps the Asian Flu.

Medicine to make you sleep
  While others make you well
Some to cure you when you're sick
  Or have a fainting spell.

Allergies are sometimes cured
  By simple good advice
The fix may not be medicine
  It's happened, more than twice.

Time could be a medicine
  I'm sure it's been revealed
Mother Nature has the skill
  And grows flowers in the field.

When you're blue, and feeling low
  Your body needs a lift
Your medicine is the Bible
  God's free word, it's a gift.

7-22-09

NUTRITION

Nutrition in the food we eat
  It keeps us well and strong
Many are the vitamins
  The list is very long.

"Variety is the spice of life"
  In stories, I've been told
Nutrition comes in many forms
  It could be hot or cold.

Vitamins will fill the gap
  Not found in what you eat
Take advice, Don't over do
  To make your needs complete.

Once found good, now they find bad
  Like vinegar and honey
Try to sell you miracle cures
  And take away your money.

7-22-09

IMPUTED

Palm Sunday, as Jesus came in sight
  Crowds threw palm leaves in His path
The same group soon condemned Him
  With their wickedness and wrath.

This is called imputed
  When encouraged by your peers
Took away the life of Jesus
  And made short all of His years.

The Bible tells the story
  Of how he was deceived
Turned love to hate by followers
  Forgot what they once believed.

7-25-09

ADORATION

Some worship unsung heroes
  Who they consider model roles
Admire all the things achieved
  And what their future holds.

This don't compare to Christ, God's Son
  That most would like to be
Our hero, friend and advocate
  He died to make us free.

Needing someone to adore
  Beside your loving mate
Seek the one with power
  He'll open St. Peter's gate.

7-23-09

YOUR TONGUE

Hearsay could distort the facts
  Plus gossip makes things worse
Truth, left out, could cause much pain
  When hearsay you disperse.

STOP - Think twice before you speak
  Don't put your mouth in gear
What comes out, and what you say
  May not be music to my ear.

Your tongue can be a weapon
  It's not a pen or sword
Happy thoughts that you share with all
  Will strike a happy chord.

7-22-09

326

INVENTION

An invention could be anything
  That improves the bottom line
Gadgets, tools, and who knows what
  Makes better, yours and mine.

Complicated, or just plain simple
  Patterns, make them yours
Many thoughts, on many things
  Is what your mind explores.

A thinking cap is needed
  It don't matter what the size
Imagination helps the cause
  Since it is given many tries.

If you wait, you could lose out
  Someone else had thoughts the same
Hesitation made you lose
  While others made the gain.

7-22-09

GRAVITY

Gravity, an unseen force
  That keeps us anchored down
The opposite, is up in space
  Where all things float around.

What a strange world this would be
  If no things were held down
Dinner plates could hold no food
  And kings could wear no crown.

All travel would be jet propelled
  Our shoes would have no wear
Many things would not exist
  And some won't need much care.

God created gravity
  To hold things in their place
Man defies this unseen force
  And travels into space.

7-22-09

My sister Louise, myself, and my brother-
in-law Larry, sometime in the 1980's.

GROUCH

Old Mr. Scrooge was called a grouch
  By all who knew him well
The Devil had him in his hand
  To welcome him to hell.

God sent three ghosts to change him
  Made him different from the past
Now he welcomes Santa Claus
  Was set straight, by the cast.

The ghosts were sent by Jesus
  That made him see the light
Now he says "Merry Christmas"
  Not once, but every night.

7-23-09

SPECTACLE

My way might seem a spectacle
  Cause my joy is in the Lord
Humor is my additive
  That I can most afford.

When God comes to take me home
  There will be a smile upon my face
I'm sure to be a winner
  When this time I'm in first place.

Spectacles are sometimes rude
  I hope it is not me
Life's too short to wear a frown
  Just hang around, and see.

7-23-09

PERSUASION

Some people need persuasion
  To do the thing that's right
Get rid of old bad habits
  Their effort might be slight.

Persistence is the only way
  When you try to make your point
Resistance, you will always find
  That might seem out of joint.

Examples are convincing
  For those with any doubt
This won't hurt the feelings
  Of those you want to tout.

Keep a smile upon your face
  When there's difficulty to persuade
In time the dark will see the light
  Of the effort you have made.

7-24-09

INDIFFERENT

Self-inclined and grouchy
  Indifferent you are called
The situation matters not
  Worked fine, until you stalled.

How you got the way you are
  When young, perhaps were spoiled
Satisfied your most desires
  Made sure your squeaks got oiled.

Up in age, with most friends lost
  Now realize you must change
Get rid of old bad habits
  Your life, must rearrange.

When God calls you home, it might be soon
  You'll want Him on your side
Bad deeds, you ask forgiveness
  Must be humble, lose your pride.

8-8-09

FANTASY

Laden with a fantasy
  Of what you'd like to be
Imagination will run wild
  To be the one you envy.

Could be you're not satisfied
  With someone like yourself
Look around, give praise to God
  That you're not Santa's elf.

When you come back down to earth
  And face reality
Reflections in the mirror
  Says I'm glad to be just me.

8-8-09

MIGHT

Might, could mean maybe?
  It also means, you're strong
Mighty is our God above
  To Him, that does belong.

A mite is a bug that's small in size
  Cause trouble when there's many
Spelling changes, what it is
  A mite could be a penny.

When it comes to being mighty
  Our God will show you how
Long story of the word MIGHT
  Is going to end — FOR NOW.

8-9-09

335

WISHES

Wishes are for dreamers
  Much prayer might make it so
Wanting to enjoy your life
  Your hopes, God will bestow.

There is no magic lamp to rub
  To make your dreams come true
Get to know how God can help
  The one and only you.

Many tales include a wish
  With stories many write
God answered that, in Bethlehem
  That silent, starry night.

8-9-09

HEALING

We can all use some healing
  At times, when we get sick
Sin will make us ill at times
  Our God can fix that quick.

Experiments eliminate, those
  Not having healing power
God sent down His only Son
  Our sins, he will devour.

Remedies to make us well
  Prescribed with medication
Prayer now found to be a help
  The AMA now gives Ovation.

8-9-09

337

MEMORY

Memory, and how it's stored
  Computers and brains compete
Any alone, don't have a chance
  Machines have it complete.

Thoughts could be a billion
  Stored, in a tiny chip
It tells you how to make things go
  So put away the whip.

No matter how smart man can get
  He still needs God to thank
A life that's filled with all good things
  Is like money in the bank.

8-9-09

TOGETHER

It's great to know you have a friend
　Who agrees with many of your thoughts
It proves that you are not alone
　When handling all unseen sorts.

Most times, we need a second view
　This input, we all need
Togetherness will do that job
　With bottom line agreed.

This should be our attitude
　With Jesus and our God
Together we'll have enjoyment
　On all the paths we trod.

8-9-09

TRUTH OR CONSEQUENCE

Truth or consequence was the game
  When "TWISTING" was the rage
Our loving God is a jealous God
  Written first upon His page.

If you sin without repent
  The Devil will take over
There will be NO heaven
  Or luscious fields of clover.

You can avoid the consequence
  And look into God's truth
Or shovel coal, way down in hell
  Reserved for all the uncouth.

8-9-09

FIRE

When controlled, it's most enjoyed
  It keeps us warm, when cold
Rapid oxidation it's called
  In many stories told.

Much destruction will take place
  When it gets out of hand
Times when weather dries things out
  All fires will be banned.

When we leave this world behind
  Cremation if desired
Now your soul will meet our Lord
  Just ashes left when fires.

Down in hell the fires burn
  Fed by repeated sinners
Up in heaven, there's no such thing
  Since God made us all winners.

8-11-09

SUPPORT

Support has many meanings
  Tall buildings put in place
This could be most anything
  Except if you're in space.

Wages earned will help support
  A family and a wife
Support you need, when you retire
  That lasts throughout your life.

Suspenders support your drooping pants
  Need support to fill your needs
Some supports help to keep you young
  And help you with your deeds.

Our loving God will give support
  Until our life will end
This should be our outlook
  Cause Christ Jesus is our friend.

8-11-09

WORDS

The dictionary has many words
  We use them every day
Definitions, sometimes many
  Looks like they're here to stay.

Many words that we all use
  Come from a foreign soil
French, Greek, and others
  Could make your knowledge boil.

Meanings changed in spelling
  Examples = TO TWO TOO
Complicated is our language
  And these are just a few.

Expression often plays the part
  Of how a word is used
Could be repeated many times
  When it becomes abused.

8-11-09

RIVERS, CREEKS AND STREAMS

Creeks and streams flow into rivers
  That empty in the sea
Many have a lot of fish
  Grown there, for you and me.

Tributaries they are called
  That drain the snow and rain
In storms the process may be slow
  Then felt, the flooding pain.

Rivers large will transport things
  To places of their need
Many companies use this way
  The savings are – indeed.

Mother Nature, led by God
  Will find a place that's low
In time might be a river
  Depending on the flow.

8-11-09

ELEVATION

Elevation plays the part
  Of temperature desired
Not too hot, or not too cold
  Just right, will be admired.

Snow remains on mountain tops
  Keeps frozen, all year long
Vegetation, and all trees
  Are down where they belong.

When you're high, up in the sky
  The sun shines bright, but cold
Thermometers are placed outside
  Degrees you will be told.

Planes fly high where air is thin
  With elevation great
Oxygen will fill our needs
  Earth creatures need this state.

8-11-09

OUR SPINNING WORLD

The earth is spinning rapidly
  And yet most things stand still
This happens every night and day
  Looks like it always will.

At night, we know all darkness
  In day, light from sunshine
Both of these are one full day
  A measurement of time.

Many "MOONS", which now mean months
  How ancients would keep time
Recorded in some picture show
  Put there for yours and mine.

All activities depend on time
  It's part of how we live
Asked which one to do without
  I doubt not one you'd give.

8-13-09

CAPACITY

Filled to capacity
  Your cup now runneth over
God takes care of all your needs
  You don't need a 4 leaf clover.

Besides all the many things
  That our great God will supply
Are the promises of heaven
  On that you can rely.

Simple faith is all it takes
  To enjoy these many things
His compassion, love and kindness
  Is what this message brings.

8-15-09

NUTRITION

Food we eat is loaded
  With nutrition, so they say
Diet comes first, upon a list
  Refrain from those marked gray.

Water mixed in all you eat
  Amount is great or little
Coffee, tea, and all warm drinks
  Poured from a steaming kettle.

Research says to eat most skins
  They are full of vitamins
Many known will head the list
  If so, our body grins.

Nutrition from the words of God
  Will keep you fit and young
This with food and exercise
  A style that must be sung.

8-15-09

IMPURE

Impure they rate our atmosphere
  Now falls the acid rain
Pollution rising rapidly
  Man contented, now complains.

This brought on by man himself
  There's no one else to blame
Will future generations exist
  If we continue to play this game.

Global warming is the trend
  The future sure looks dim
The outlook might be God's own way
  To make the population slim.

To reverse this situation
  That brought about this feat
Responsible, are everyone
  When in the driver's seat.

8-15-09

SECONDARY

Once considered secondary
  Cause the color of their skin
The melting pot, America
  That's how it's always been.

Much prejudice, inherited
  With thoughts to be supreme
Hard work and dedication
  Will turn your milk to cream.

Envy of the risen one
  Not lazy, from the start
If you want the same success
  You have to earn your part.

Equal and not secondary
  Those first, who ring the bell
Successful and admired
  Because they did it well.

8-15-09

QUESTIONS

Information that we do not have
  Ask questions, what is right?
Someone has the answer
  I'm sure it's not locked up tight.

Our life is full of questions
  Of how, the why and when
If you want to know the truth
  The Bible repeats this once again.

The young ask many questions
  That's how they grow and learn
Having most the answers
  Should be our most concern.

This process is forever
  Until the day we die
All this knowledge you can take
  To heaven, in the sky.

8-17-09

PRACTICE

Much knowledge have all doctors
  That keep us well and strong
A life of dedication
  Many studies, hard and long.

Yet it's called a practice
  With some decisions wrong
Most times twice is better
  To sing a happy song.

No one can be perfect
  There is only one Christ
Some try their best to imitate
  Like pulling off a heist.

Doing it right, in practice
  Will help you to excel
High above the average
  Because you do it well.

8-17-09

REPUTATION

Displaying what comes natural
  Soon will be your reputation
Meek and mild, or wildly bold
  It's you — without perfection.

Sad, not jolly, full of gloom
  Some show this every day
Avoided with not many friends
  The price they have to pay.

Attraction, that's called chemistry
  Hid well beneath your skin
Revealed, to one who likes you
  Romance thus does begin.

Your attitude sure plays the part
  That helps you to succeed
Happiness, the bottom line
  All summed up, and agreed.

8-17-09

Easter Sunday, 1965, in front of 8 Temple Rd. New
Jersey. Martha and I with our children
(L- R). Diane, Robert, Neil, Joanne, and William.

RAZZ-MA-TAZZ

The rambunctious seek much razz-ma-tazz
  The Devil hears their call
Party time, where all things go
  Makes Satan have a ball.

Cigarettes and alcohol
  Will help you speed the pace
Get involved, then be a part
  Of all who run this race.

Looking toward tomorrow
  With hope for Razz-ma-tazz
Soon worn out, beat and tired
  Fed up will all that jazz.

Single pleasures now you seek
  That will forever last
Remember your foolish acts
  While living in the past.

8-17-09

OUTLOOK

Most people have an outlook
  Not settled in their ways
Searching for Utopia
  And what its outlook says.

They keep looking for a miracle
  Wish free from all bad news
Keep hoping for much better things
  To brighten up their views.

Many find the answer
  It came from God's own truth
Refrain from old bad habits
  When activities were uncouth.

With Sun not always shining
  Learn to accept the rain
All things will be much better
  When Christ returns again.

8-17-09

RELATIONSHIP

Same blood, same genes, same everything
  Makes mother and child profound
Like a plant at harvest time
  Spring up from solid ground.

God and Jesus, a family tie
  Influential in our life
Unseen, with Holy Spirit
  United, like man and wife.

With prayer we're in God's family
  This relationship is good
Some day in heaven we'll meet Him
  A promise understood.

8-18-09

ENLIGHTEN

Missionaries have the job
  To enlighten all the world
Some times, way back in heathen land
  To make God's truth unfurled.

Not trusting and most dangerous
  These inhabitants might be
Once taught in their own language
  A-Men to victory.

Dedication in their calling
  Not all may feel this way
A lifetime of salvation
  To teach God's love, and pray.

8-19-09

HELTER SKELTER

An attitude of "I don't care"
  The brain says helter skelter
When looking for a place to hide
  Try God, you'll find a shelter.

When you've reached your low or lows
  And can't stand any more
That's the time to seek the Lord
  He'll open every door.

Scatter brain, to all you know
  Your personality needs a fix
Pray to God to change your life
  He don't play any tricks.

8-19-09

BELLIGERMENT

Resentment mixed with boredom
  Equals much belligerment
Not always did you feel this
  Most low, and feeling spend.

While you're alive, there still is time
  To change, so all can see
A loving, carefree person
  The one you'd like to be.

There will be times of sadness
  This comes to all the living
Be admired by your new approach
  With the outlook that you're giving.

8-19-09

STEADFAST

Repeating what you know is good
  You're steadfast in your ways
Good daily habits, same routine
  The outcome surely pays.

Persisting in all things you do
  Unaffected by your peers
Common sense, by you was used
  Throughout your many years.

Give an inch, don't take a yard
  Treat others with respect
When you love and compromise
  Much enjoyment you'll collect.

8-19-09

NOISEY

Illusions of the restless
  Who have nothing else to do
Annoying all each chance they get
  Their mind is in a stew.

A bad habit that is hard to break
  With momentum picks up speed
Continued many countless times
  'Til sleep will stop this deed.

Restlessness and boredom
  Together, hand in hand
Clamor with disruption
  Is the leader of the band.

8-22-09

INCONSISTENT

Inconsistent are the actions
  Most annoying to all who dwell
A wolf cry of necessities
  Echoed sounds, that come from hell.

Much attention is desired
  Since boredom has crept in
This call repeated constantly
  Makes you jump out of your skin.

Old age might be the answer
  To the problem close at hand
Not capable of many things
  Takes place, like shifting sands.

8-23-09

INDESTRUCTIBLE

Our God is indestructible
  All creation, in his power
What ever is called mighty
  To the smallest of the flower.

Jesus came to prove this so
  By miracles He did
He took away the mysteries
  Which made most of them admit.

The world should know that once you're dead
  Your spirit and soul lives on
At Easter, there is proof of this
  Now doubts and fear are gone.

8-24-09

PUNISHMENT

Nails driven through both hands and feet
  Then hung upon a tree
Excruciating pain this caused
  Hung high, so all could see.

Romans gave this punishment
  To all criminals at this time
Jesus suffered the all above
  For sins like yours and mine.

Though innocent, it was God's plan
  To send His Son to earth
To sacrifice His precious kin
  When Mary gave him birth.

His teachings and His rise from death
  Much proof was made to all
Easter sums up all the facts
  Many stories, you recall.

9-1-09

FUNCTIONS

God's creatures all have functions
  No matter what they be
Noah made his ark quite big
  With hopes all doubters would see.

Male and female of each kind
  So they could reproduce
Included were the many trees
  That supply us all with juice.

Food for all the predators
  For humans, much the same
All function with a purpose
  This cycle will remain.

Man, great with his technology
  Has changed what God has wrought
Could lead to much extinction
  Unless it's given thought.

9-5-09

VOWS

Promises before almighty God
  Are vows sincerely spoken
In time, regardless what takes place
  They never should be broken.

Marriage tops the list for vows
  Make sure your mate is right
Second thoughts should not exist
  To cause a sleepless night.

Until death, are words you said
  The affection of your feeling
Difficulties will arise at time
  Try gazing at the ceiling.

True love can withstand the many trials
  And weather every storm
Prayers to God will help bad times
  His love will keep you strong.

9-6-09

SOARING

When young, you're full of energy
　Like a lion who is roaring
Your spirit high, just like a kite
　Much like a plane, you're soaring.

As years go by, it's back to earth
　Time for your body's landing
Life's up and downs do now exist
　Rough edges now need sanding.

When you're looking for a high
　Our God will show you how
Be amazed at His great power
　Say A-men or Holy Cow.

Spirit soaring, when you're gone
　To heaven, with the King
Jesus there to greet you
　You'll hear the angels sing.

9-6-09

SHOCKING NEWS

Like electric current
  Sometimes shocking, is the news
Catastrophes around the world
  Take preference for our views.

Last minute changes are in store
  When unexpected things take place
All details will come later
  From reporters on the case.

Special programs fill you in
  And bring you up to date
Other news is put aside
  For this you'll have to wait.

Each new day, not like the rest
  New happenings there will be
Live television at the scene
  For all of us to see.

9-6-09

SMOKING

Smoking cigarettes, a bad, bad habit
  Most times, it's hard to break
Promises that you can quit
  Lots of money companies take.

"COLD TURKEY" is the only way
  Much prayer will make it so
Don't believe all ads you hear
  They'll take away your dough.

Strong willpower is the method
  It is the only way
I know, because I used to smoke
  My cure is here to stay.

Just like an alcoholic
  A smoker you'll always be
It takes just one to start again
  Say NO! and you'll be free.

9-6-09

THE MOON

Once a month the moon gets full
  Then tides are extra high and low
The rocks along the shore line
  Hide many worms below.

Other times you have to dig
  For bait beneath the sand
The quickest way to fill your need
  With holes dug from dry land.

Storms at sea will come ashore
  And flood when the moon is full
This happened many times before
  Because the moon has pull.

Time was kept by American Indians
  They said "Many moons ago"
Soon, there will be excursion trips
  Perhaps you want to go?

9-8-09

REGENERATION

At times, when crabs will lose a claw
  Regeneration will take place
Soon a new one will appear
  Like new to feed its face.

Prosthetics help man walk again
  When he has lost a leg
Technology made this possible
  No need for him to beg.

The need to lift your spirit
  When you're feeling low
Our gracious God is there to help
  He heals, that's good to know.

Don't worry what you lost in life
  In heaven, your body soars
Souls don't have any aches or pains
  They're free from earthly flaws.

9-12-09

REDEEMED

When you are a saver
  Many coupons you redeemed
The savings total quite a lot
  More than you ever dreamed.

Stamps, reductions of all kinds
  It pays more than you think
Your budget gets a breather
  Since there is no more red ink.

Sinners were redeemed by Christ
  It was God's only way
Sacrificed His only Son
  With prayer of thanks "I SAY"

Once you are in heaven
  No need to be redeemed
Your shining health will wear a crown
  Just like a star that beamed.

9-13-09

AUSTRALIA

A place that is so far away
  "DOWN UNDER" is its name
Australia holds this title
  With seasons much the same.

Accents you hear give hints
  Of where the person's from
Familiar objects have different names
  Are just a few, from some.

Just like us, with all we have
  Australia ranks up high
Some day I would like to visit
  For this, I'd have to fly.

9-13-09

REFLECTION

Others look at what you do
  Your reflection is what they see
A sunny disposition
  Or a grouch, that you might be.

Each morn, the mirror reflects your face
  It may look tired and worn
Other times it's cheerful
  Feel like tooting your own horn.

As Christians we have much to do
  To beam a lovable expression
Having faith, to act this way
  For all to know, this session.

Judgement from your peers made known
  It's either good or bad
God will help you live with joy
  He has, and always had.

9-15-09

CHURCH

Church, a place to worship God
   Christians, others and Jews
Some follow teachings of God's Son
   And tell of His "Good News"

Cathedral, barn, or any place
   They join in fellowship
Make plans for all the next events
   Perhaps it is a trip?

Most times all meet on weekends
   And some during the week
A constant drive their motive
   The Bible's wisdom they all seek.

A church is just a meeting place
   Where two or more will gather
Many never go to church
   Do other things they'd rather.

9-15-09

ARCHANGELS

Archangels are the chosen ones
  Picked from all the rest
They're ranked above the others
  When God made their spirit blest.

They lead the many angels
  That do all God's good deeds
Petitions, filled with lots of prayers
  That take care of all our needs.

They have so many things to do
  It sure is hard to count
A job that satisfies His flock
  Much work, as tasks will mount.

9-20-09

My beautiful wife, Martha during her
struggle with cancer, 2007.

COMPASSION

When dealing with compassion
  Interception comes with love
Thoughts and words, our God did give
  From His mansion up above.

He says "BE SLOW TO ANGER"
  Even when there seems no cure
In time He'll give the peace you ask
  With love and grace that's pure.

"Forgive me God," when I don't act
  With understanding love
You answered prayers to make things right
  And helped that lonesome dove.

9-25-09

CONDITION

An object, whether old or new
  When its condition is kept good
The lasting joy of using it
  The effort understood.

Condition is used describing things
  The dictionary says it's so
A big list of many uses
  For people on the go.

Conditions of the weather
  They will constantly make change
Plans for things on sunshine days
  Your time must rearrange.

9-21-09

PERPETUAL

Perpetual is forever
 Not like the falling rain
There is no need for energy
 Its function to sustain.

Man hopes some day to discover
 The perpetual motion machine
Solar power might be used
 While others, still a dream.

Perpetual is the action
 Of our almighty God
Heaven is a form of this
 When He gives us the nod.

9-27-09

GOOD DEEDS

In my room, on the wall
  A plaque I can't ignore
It says "God opens windows"
  When at times He shuts a door.

This happened many times before
  So many I can recall
This aids in testimony
  That enlightens one and all.

The need to be reminded
  How God can fill our needs
Remember that young Boy Scout
  When you perform good deeds.

9-26-09

DISABLED

When classified disabled
  Cause some functions don't exist
You get much recognition
  Since there are many on that list.

Devices there are plenty
  To keep you from a fall
Parking places, lots of signs
  Made plain, and seen by all.

Ramps for those in wheel chairs
  Helps of many kings
Thanks to our technology
  Praise God! For inventive minds.

9-28-09

SOUL AND SOLE

Quite different than the soul of man
  A sole, that is a fish
This includes the flounder
  That makes a tasty dish.

A scavenger, who eats all things
  That lie along the bottom
Pollution filled with PCB's
  When eaten, you have got 'em.

Fish I'm sure don't have a soul
  And don't know of our heaven
Steal our bait and don't get hooked
  May think, it's Lucky Seven?

10-2-09

TALENT

Humans blessed with talent
  A gift from our great God
Put aside, and never used
  Until he gives the nod.

Size don't really matter
  Perform and you'll stand tall
It's good to know we have a God
  To catch us if we fall.

Admired for your blessing
  And the many things you do
Be thankful for the gifts bestowed
  On the one and only you.

10-9-09

MISERY

Misery likes company
  While sympathy is sharing sorrow
Friends are there to cheer you up
  For a brighter new tomorrow.

At painful times you're miserable
  Reflecting all your hurts
Matters not what sex you are
  It could be pants or skirts.

Christ was inflected with agony
  When hung upon the cross
Rose again, from what seemed death
  Thus made our sins a loss.

Misery will be no more
  When we make our final bow
We'll be free from all our worldly pain
  Our Lord did show us how.

10-3-09

CONNECTION

We have the best connection
  Jesus Christ, God's Son, our Lord
Saved us from our worldly sins
  At a price all can afford.

No matter just how hard we try
  We'll never reach perfection
There is one Christ, and only one
  We worship with affection.

Our God made all this possible
  When He sacrificed His Son
He snatched us from the Devil's hand
  Now we have a victory, won.

10-12-09

DELIVERANCE

Deliverance was a movie back in 1973
  It was a show of shows
A tale which had much violence
  That included dueling banjos.

It showed the many sins of man
  There were also lots of thrills
Canoes, white water, filled with rocks
  At times there were some spills.

Sworn to keep all secrets
  Of horrors that took place
Once again, returned to work
  With shame wiped off each face.

Only God will be the judge
  Of things that happened there
Put aside their tales of woe
  With stories they won't share.

10-12-09

PREMONITION

There are many premonitions
  Of what we have in store
When you believe the word of God
  Premonitions, you need no more.

All of us have great ideas
  Of what the future holds
Only in time we will find out
  Like a cure for common colds.

Prophets predict things to come
  Based on their premonition
Many times they will be true
  Because of God's permission.

10-13-09

TRUST

Jump and I will catch you
  Words the Father said, To Trust
Frightened 'til safe in his arms
  Assurance in a must.

It is the same with Father God
  With faith, we must believe
He'll catch us when we have a fall
  He never will deceive.

The many times I needed God
  He was close by my side
Saved me from the depths of hell
  He'll always be my guide.

12-9-09

My son Bill's wedding, 2005. Seated L – R: Jonathan, Joanna and David Urton. Standing L – R: David Urton, Diane Gartner Urton, Martha Gartner, Julia Bachman, Willam Gartner, Kathy Prugh Gartner, Harold Gartner, and JoAnne Gartner.